Words of Life

This publication was designed for pre-adolescent students (9 to 11 years old - 4th, 5th and 6th graders).

STUDENT ACTIVITY WORKSHEETS
Year 2

Corresponds to Year 2 of the cycle of three years of WORDS OF LIFE (pre-adolescent Children) lesson books.

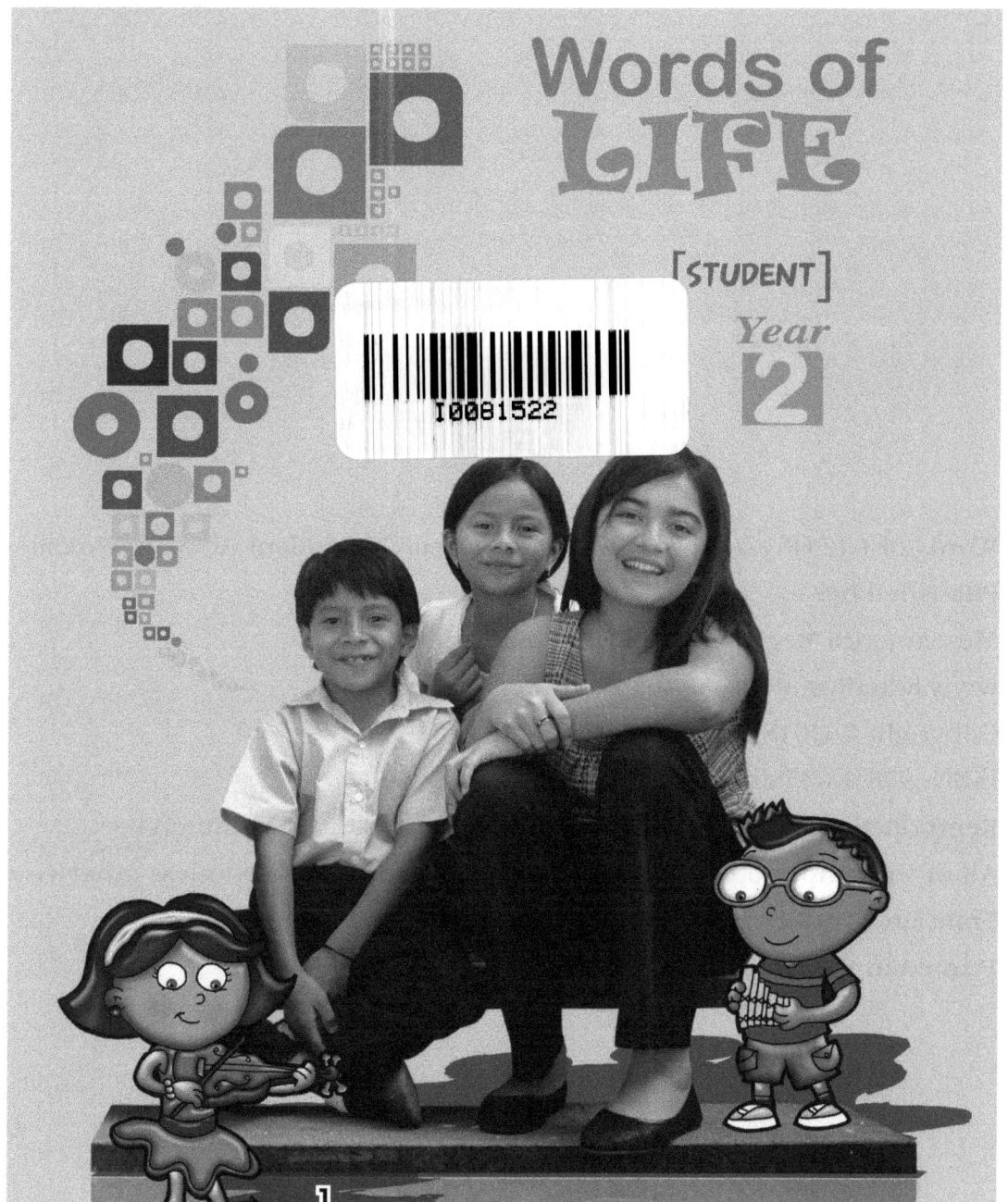

Words of Life (Pre-adolescent Children), Year 2 - Student Activity Worksheets

Published by:

Mesoamerica Region Discipleship Ministries

www.SdmiResources.MesoamericaRegion.org

Copyright © 2018 - All rights reserved

ISBN: 978-1-63580-117-0

All of the scripture verses quoted are from the NIV Bible unless otherwise stated.

Translated into English from Spanish by: Bethany Cyr

Printed in the United States

Mesoamerica Region

Table of Contents

NOTE: Teachers, please be aware that some of the worksheets need what is printed on both sides of the page. If you are making copies, and cannot copy on both sides of the paper, you may want to make copies of both pages and glue them together or give your students extra time to color the back of the worksheet.
On another note about copying, rather that making photocopies from the book, it may be easier to print from the digital copy that can be found at our resource site here: www.SdmiResources.MesoamericaRegion.org   Search for the name of the book.

FIRST THINGS FIRST

What do you think about RULES?

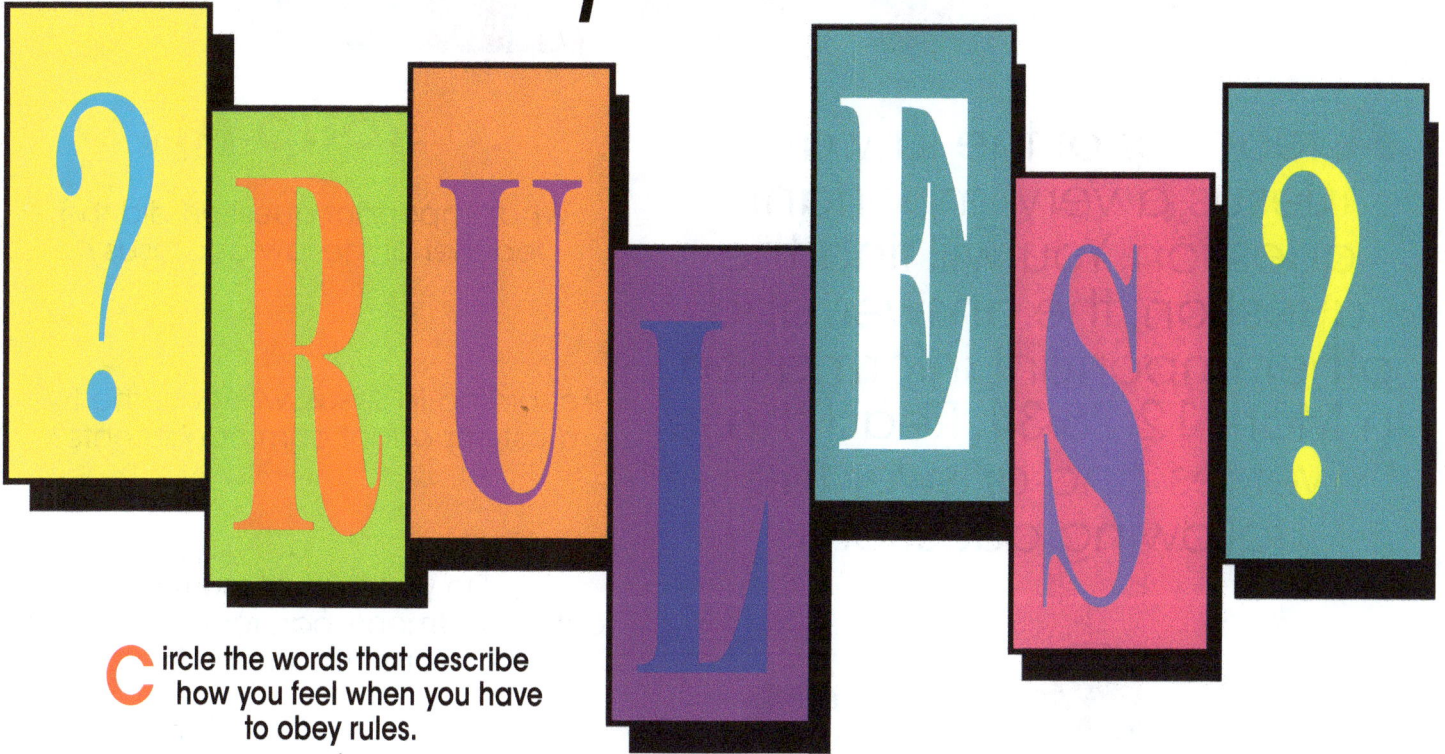

C ircle the words that describe how you feel when you have to obey rules.

ANGRY

I HATE RULES

We Need More

Bad

BORED

Good

I DON'T CARE

Happy!

Limited

EXCITED!

Not Restricted

They're Necessary

JESUS CHANGES THE RULES?

A teacher of the law asked Jesus a very important question. You will find the question, the answer, and other important information in Mark 12:28-34. Read these verses and answer the following questions.

Group A:

What important question did the teacher of the law ask Jesus?

According to Jesus, what are the two most important commandments?

Do you think these two commandments can replace the Ten Commandments ?

Group B:

In what way should we love God?

What is more important to God than offerings and sacrifices?

How can we know if the teacher of the law understood what Jesus said?

What idols do people worship today?

IDOLS

Rule Nº1

You shall have no other gods before me.

(Exodus 20:3)

Rule Nº2

You shall not make for yourself an image in the form of anything

(Exodus 20:4a)

HAVE WE CHANGED THE RULES?

What Should I Do?

Write a letter to God expressing your love for Him. Tell Him what you will do to put him first in your life.

Dear God:

_____

_____

_____

_____

_____

_____

_____

_____

_____

_____

_____

_____

_____

_____

_____

_____

_____

"'Love the Lord your God with all your heart and with all your soul and with all your mind and with all your strength.' The second is this: 'Love your neighbor as yourself.' There is no commandment greater than these."
(Mark 12:30-31)

POWER OF WORDS

What does the Bible say about the things I say?

This alien is sending a report to the planet Marsatplutus about the way that the inhabitants of Earth respect each other. He heard that a book called the Bible teaches that humans must be respectful through words. Read the following verses, and help the alien write a brief report.

REPORT FOR MARSATPLUTUS

Date: _____

Sent by: _____

_____

Message:

Matthew 5:33-37; 12:35-37; Ephesians 4:29; Colossians 3:8-9.

The BIBLE says . . .

Answer these questions:

What does the third commandment tell us about how we should respect God? (Exodus 20:7)

What did the Hebrews call God?

What does "Jehovah" mean?

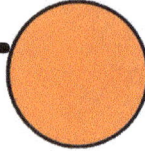

What did Jesus tell people about taking God's name in vain? (Matthew 5:33-37; 12:35-37).

In what ways do people today use the name of God in vain?

What did Paul tell the Christians about the way they spoke? (Ephesians 4:29; Colossians 3:8-9)

In what way do people misuse words today?

People differ from other creatures created by God because they have the ability to communicate through words. Unfortunately, many people misuse the gift God has given us. Below you will find some improper ways that language is used. Find the words that match the definitions and complete the crossword puzzle.

MISUSE OF OUR ABILITY TO SPEAK

Horizontal

1. Words that are said with the intention of hurting someone.
2. Intense emotion caused by something negative.
3. Negative comment about another person.
4. Indecent and obscene.
5. Expression of dissatisfaction.

Vertical

6. Act of lying to damage the reputation of someone.
7. Rumor about someone.
8. Cruel taunting to offend or harm someone.
9. Disdain or lack of appreciation for something or someone.
10. Indignation and uncontrollable anger.

Evaluate Your Words!

Read the sentences, and check the column that describes the way your friends talk. Then, with a different color, mark the ones that describe how you talk. In what area(s) do you need to improve?

	ALWAYS	SOMETIMES	NEVER
You use words that humiliate others.			
When you're with your friends, you criticize others.			
You tell bad jokes & rude stories.			
You say bad words.			
You use the name of God in vain.			
You say nice things about others.			
You tell the truth.			

anger
contempt
gossip
slander
insults
sarcasm
criticism
complaint
vulgar
rage

A Prayer About the Words I Use

TEACHER: Father, we know you want our conversations to be pure.

STUDENTS: Help us to keep our language clean, avoiding bad words.

TEACHER: We know you do not want us to lie.

STUDENTS: Help us to always tell the truth.

TEACHER: Remind us that your name is holy.

STUDENTS: Help us to respect your Holy name.

TEACHER: We often hear humiliating words and know that they cause harm to others.

STUDENTS: Help us to use our words to encourage others.

ALL: We want to speak in a way that glorifies you.

TEACHER: The Bible tells us that we must honor the name of God.

ALL: "You shall not misuse the name of the Lord your God, for the Lord will not hold anyone guiltless who misuses his name." (Exodus 20: 7)

TEACHER: The Word of God tells us to encourage others with our words.

STUDENTS: "Do not let any unwholesome talk come out of your mouths, but only what is helpful for building others up according to their needs, that it may benefit those who listen." (Ephesians 4:29).

ALL: God, help us to honor you with the words we say. Amen.

A SPECIAL DAY

Imagine that you are a reporter or newscaster for the Capernaum News.

You are assigned to interview and write a report on one of the following topics: the Pharisees; the disciples of Jesus; the man with the shriveled hand; Jesus.

Journalist's Notes
CAPERNAUM NEWS

Date: _____

Place: _____

Journalist's Name: _____

Topic: _____

What do you do on the Lord's Day?

Make a list of the activities that you do on Sundays.	TIME SPENT	TYPE OF ACTIVITY
_____	_____	_____
_____	_____	_____
_____	_____	_____
_____	_____	_____
_____	_____	_____
_____	_____	_____
_____	_____	_____
_____	_____	_____

OD DOGO GSTINH

PSIRHOW DGO

SETR

Re-arrange the letters to discover three kinds of activities that you can do to glorify God on the Sabbath.

The Day of the Lord

Do you think these young people keep the Sabbath?

Maria goes to a nursing home every Sunday to visit the people who live there.

Thomas likes basketball and Sundays are the only time he has time to play. So he spends the afternoon playing basketball near his house with his friends.

Alicia takes care of her neighbor's children on Saturday nights. She returns home very late and she is too tired to go to Sunday school the next day. She says that Sunday is her day of rest.

Michael's friend asked him to go to the park on Sunday. Michael wanted his friend to know Jesus, so he invited his friend to go to church first, then they'll go to the park together.

Lucy goes to Sunday School every Sunday. But Lucy likes to talk with her friends and sometimes she's so busy talking that she doesn't listen to what the teacher says.

Andy decided to go to his friend's house after church so that he can help his friend clean the patio.

(Mark 12:30-31)

"'Love the Lord your God

with all your heart,

and with all your soul,

and with all your mind

and with all your strength.'

the second is this:

'Love your neighbor

as yourself.

There is no commandment

greater than these.'"

(Mark 12:30-31)

**(1 John 4:9-10)
This is how
God showed**

**his love
among us:**

**He sent his one
and only Son**

**into the world
that we**

**might live
through him.**

**This is love:
not that we
loved God,**

**but that
he loved us**

**and sent
his Son**

**as an atoning
sacrifice**

for our sins.

(1 John 4:9-10)

Cut off the strip with the Bible verses and cut out the white window in the upper right corner. Fold the sheet along the dotted line, and glue the side edges together. Insert the text strip until the words appear in the window. Repeat the Bible verse, phrase by phrase, sliding the strip up to check to see if you are saying it correctly.

WE NEED OUR PARENTS

HONOR

Honor: to treat someone with respect and special attention.

Who?

What?

Why?

_____ will be

honored for _____

_____

_____

Date:_____

(Signature)_____

_____ will be

honored for _____

_____

_____

Date:_____

(Signature)_____

_____ will be

honored for _____

_____

_____

Date:_____

(Signature)_____

**God tells
preteens
(Exodus 20:12)**

**Jesus tells
preteens
(Luke 2:51-52;
John 19:25-27)**

**Paul tells
preteens
(Ephesians 6:1-3)**

THEY

HAVE

THING

ALL

SOME

TO SAY !

Preteens tell their parents

Preteens tell other preteens

How can I show RESPECT to my parents?

Rate yourself by checking the appropriate column	ALMOST ALWAYS	SOME TIMES	ALMOST NEVER
I speak well of my parents when I'm with my friends.			
I obey my parents.			
I have a good opinion of my parents.			
I treat my parents the way I would like them to treat me.			
I keep my room clean.			
I ask my parents permission before I do something.			
I obey my parents without complaining.			
I express my love and affection to my parents.			

Coupon valid until _____

Because I love and respect my parents, this week I will

_____

_____

_____

_____

Signature

WHAT DO YOU SEE?

My Favorite TV Shows

Make a list of your five favorite TV shows or movies.

1.
2.
3.
4.
5.

Rate your five favorite TV shows or movies.

Nonviolent   Very Violent

0   1   2   3

What the Bible says about Anger and Violence

Group 1: Read Exodus 20:13.
1. What is murder?
2. Why do you think God established a command against murder?

Group 2: Read Matthew 5:21-22.
1. Who deserves to be judged?
2. Why did Jesus say that anger deserves judgment?

Group 3: Read James 1:19-20.
1. Why did James warn Christians to avoid anger?
2. What does James suggest that we do?

Write one or more laws against violence for the city of Megapolis.

Law N°_____ for the city of Megapolis.

_____

_____

_____

M

I AM SPECIAL

what are they selling?

Make a list of 5 commercials or advertisements that you like.

RATING

_____   _____

_____   _____

_____   _____

_____   _____

_____   _____

Rate them with a 0 if they do not promote sexual immorality as a way to sell the product, or with a ? if they do.

23

The Bible says

The Holy Bible

GROUP 1:
Genesis 1:27-31; 2:20-24

- According to the Bible, where did sex come from?
- How would you describe God's attitude about sex?
- What makes you think that?

GROUP 2:
Exodus 20:14; Matthew 5:27-28; Romans 1:18, 26-32

What warnings does the Bible give about sex?

GROUP 3:
1 Corinthians 10:13; 1 Thessalonians 4: 1-5

What can we do when we are tempted to sin?

24

IF IT'S NOT YOURS, LEAVE IT ALONE !

Do Not Touch !

GRADES

English	0 0
History	0 0
Spanish	0
Physical Ed.	0

Make a list of five objects that you would not miss if they were stolen.

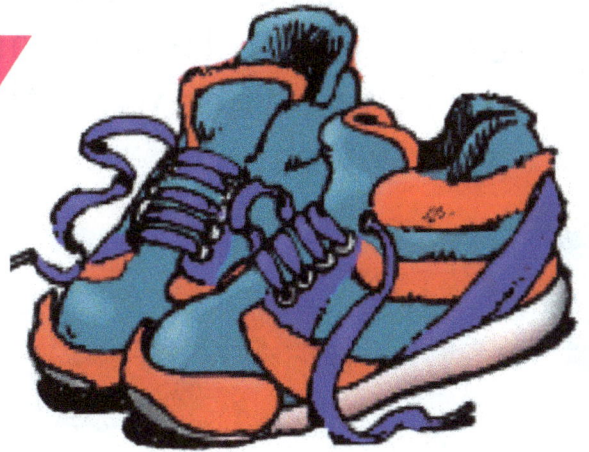

Make a list of five objects that you would NOT want to be stolen.

To Steal or Not to Steal?

What does the Bible say?

Steal: to take someone else's property without permission.
Restitution: return what was stolen or pay the owner what the stolen item was worth.

1. What is God's law about stealing? (Exodus 20:15).

2. If we want something, what should we do instead of stealing it? (Ephesians 4:28)

3. According to the concordance in your Bible, how many times does the word "steal" appear in the Bible?

4. If a preteen steals someone's watch, what should they do to restore the damage?

26

Steal
Copy
Defraud or Swindle
Defame
Vandalism
Filch
DIFFER
TYPES
STEAL

Steal: to take something that is not yours without paying for it.

Copy: to use another person's ideas as if they were your own.

Defraud or Swindle: to take something from someone by being tricky or deceitful.

Defame: to discredit someone, verbally or in writing, to damage their reputation.

Vandalism: to damage someone else's property on purpose.

Filch: to steal, especially something of small value.

ENT
OF
ING

IS THIS STEALING?

Miss Julia, who almost never leaves her house, asked John to cut the grass in her garden, and she pays him for the work. To save time, every week John only cuts the areas that she can see from her windows, and every two weeks he cuts all the grass. He says he does this so that he doesn't have to charge others as much. Is John stealing?

Silvia broke off her engagement with Joel. He is so angry that he decided to spread rumors about her. Is Joel stealing? What is he stealing?

Every time Andy needs money, he goes to his father's room and takes the coins he finds on the night stand or in his father's pockets. Is Andy stealing?

Alice and Sofia went to the store and bought milk for Sofia's mother. On the way home, Sofia gave Alice a chocolate.
"Thanks for buying me a chocolate," said Alice. "I am very hungry".
"I didn't buy it," Sofia said laughing. "That store charges way more than it should, so I took it without paying." Is Sofia stealing?

Tom asked Daniel if he had finished the math project that his group had to do. When Daniel said yes, Tom asked him if he could borrow it. "I knew you were going to finish it. I was so busy that I didn't get it done. Can I borrow yours for a few minutes." Is Tom stealing?

Rita got angry because Angela did not want to lend her the music CD she was listening to. Without anyone noticing, Rita took the CD from Angela's bag, broke it and put it back in the same place. "This will teach you how to share," Rita said. Did Rita steal? How?

The Consequences of STEALING

The consequences of defrauding are:

The consequences of defaming are:

The consequences of filching are:

The consequences of stealing are:

The consequences of copying are:

The consequences of vandalizing are:

How Can You Avoid the Consequences?

Lesson 8

LYING BRINGS CONSEQUENCES

Be Careful With Lying!

Ananias and his wife Sapphira sold a piece of land. Then, they agreed to keep part of the money for themselves and give the rest to the apostles.

Peter said to Ananias, "Ananias, how is it that Satan has enter into your heart and that you have lied to the Holy Spirit, keeping some of the money for yourself? Did not everything belong to you before you sold it? You have not lied just to us, but to God."

When Ananias heard this, he fell dead instantly. Great fear seized all who heard what had happened. Then some young men came forward, wrapped the body and took it to be buried.

About three hours later, his wife arrived, not knowing what had happened. Peter asked her, "Tell me, is this the price that you sold your land for?"

"That's right," she replied, "that's the price."

Then Peter said to her, "Why did you agree to test the Spirit of the Lord? Look! Here come the young men who have just buried your husband, and they will bury you also."

At that moment she fell dead at Peter's feet. The young men entered and took her to bury her with her husband.

(Acts 5:1-10)

WOULD YOU BELIEVE

SITUATIONS

Write a situation that is an example of each kind of lie. We did the first one as an example.

White Lies:
to change or omit a small detail, or lie about a seemingly insignificant issue.

Emily was excited to show her new blouse to Kathy. "It's very pretty," Kathy said, not wanting to make Emily feel bad. But in reality, Kathy didn't like Emily's new blouse.

Gossip:
to reveal personal or false information about someone.

Defamation:
to falsely say something about someone to destroy their reputation.

Not Telling the Truth:
to keep secret a truth that we should tell.

Exaggeration:
to make something seem much better or much worse than it really is.

Perjury:
to say something false after swearing (promising) to tell the truth.

THESE LIES?

Consequences

Write a consequence for each situation that the person who is lying may have to face. We did the first one as an example.

Emily will not look pretty wearing the blouse. Kathy will feel bad when she sees Emily wear the blouse and she thinks it looks good. Kathy may also hear negative comments that others make about Emily's blouse.

TRUTH

THE TEST OF

Read each sentence and decide if it is true or false. Write "T" if it is true, and "F" if it is false.

Then, read the phrases again, this time saying "I" instead of "many preteens". Use a different color pen/pencil and again write "T" for true and "F" for false as it relates to you.

How do you rate?

1. Many preteens sometimes lie to their parents.

2. Many preteens tell the truth.

3. Many preteens have cheated or copied someone else's assignments or tests.

4. Many preteens gossip.

5. Many preteens sometimes exaggerate the truth.

6. If they know the truth, many preteens prefer to tell the truth.

7. Many preteens sometimes cheat others.

8. Many preteens damage other people's reputations.

9. Many preteens forgive people who lied about them.

10. Many preteens apologize for the lies they have told.

Therefore each of you must put off falsehood and speak truthfully to your neighbor, for we are all members of one body. (Ephesians 4:25)

32

DON'T ENVY

SLAVES OF THE CODE

Write the steps that a person goes through from wanting something, to committing a crime to get it.

i want what you have!

1. Define the word "greed".

2. What did God say about greed in the Ten Commandments? (Exodus 20:17)

3. Why would coveting be rejecting God? (Philippians 4:10-13, 19)

4. What did Jesus say about possessions? (Matthew 6: 19-21)

5. Why aren't the following ideas about possessions correct?

   A. Everyone has the right to enjoy all the good things in life equally.

   B. We all have the right to enjoy equally what others have.

   C. The more possessions we have, the happier we will be.

6. What is the remedy for greed? (Hebrews 13:5)

"Keep your lives free from the love of money and be content with what you have". (Hebrews 13:5a)

Lesson 10

JOB'S SUFFERING

Father of four children dies in a plane crash.

Three women die in an unusual elevator accident.

WHY DO BAD THINGS HAPPEN TO CHRISTIANS?

A house is destroyed by fire.

A nine year old boy suffers from leukemia.

AN ELDERLY MAN WHO SURVIVED A TRAIN ACCIDENT DIES OF BRAIN CANCER.

An earthquake destroys hundreds of homes.

The authorities imprison a teenager.

35

What Happened to Job?

In the land of Uz lived a good and honest man named Job. He honored God and kept away from evil. He had seven sons and three daughters; and he owned 7,000 sheep, 3,000 camels, 500 yokes of oxen and 500 donkeys, in addition to having many servants. He was the most important man in the East.

His sons used to celebrated their birthdays with feasts in their homes and they invited their sisters to eat and drink with them. After those feasts, Job arranged for them to be purified. Rising early in the morning, he offered burnt offerings for each of them, thinking, "Perhaps my children have sinned and they have cursed God in their hearts." This was Job's regular custom.

One day the angels presented themselves before God, and Satan was with them. And God asked Satan: "Where have you come from?"

"From roaming throughout the earth." Satan replied.

"What do you think of Job, my faithful servant? There is no one on earth like him. He is a blameless and honorable man, who always obeys me and avoids doing evil," said the Lord.

"Job honors you for a good reason. You protect him, his family, everything he owns and you have blessed everything he has done. But, if you extend your hand and strike everything he has, you will surely see him curse you to your face," Satan replied.

"Very well, do what you want with everything he has, but do not touch Job," God said.

One day, while Job's children were celebrating at the elder brother's house, a messenger came to Job and said,

"Some bandits attacked us and stole all the animals! They killed all the servants and only I escaped to bring you the news."

The messenger was still talking when another messenger arrived and told Job,

"The fire of God fell from heaven and killed all the sheep and the shepherds! I only escaped to warn you."

Another messenger arrived and said:

"Three raiding parties of Chaldean bandits attacked us, killed the servants and took away the camels. I just escaped!

The third messenger was speaking, when another messenger arrived and said:

"Your children were celebrating, when suddenly a mighty desert wind came and demolished the house. All who were in the house died! Only I escaped to give you the news."

When Job heard this, he stood up, tore his cloak and shaved his head in sadness. Then, bowing to the ground, he worshiped God and said,

"Naked I came from my mother's womb, and naked I will depart. The Lord gave and the Lord has taken away; May the name of the Lord be praised!"

Once again the angels presented themselves before the Lord, and Satan with them, and God said to Satan,

"Have you seen my servant Job? He is still a good and honest man, even though you convinced me to let you do him harm for no reason."

"Skin for skin!" Satan replied. "A man will give everything that he has for his own life. But stretch out your hand, strike his flesh and bones and you will surely see him curse you to your face.

"Very well, he is in your hands; but you must spare his life," replied God.

So Satan covered Job's whole body with sores. Then Job sat on ashes and all day he scratched himself with a piece of pottery.

His wife told him,

"Why do you insist on behaving righteously? Better curse God and die!"

"You are talking like a foolish woman. Will we receive from God only the good, and not accept the bad?" Job replied.

Despite everything that had happened to him, Job did not sin against God. (Job 1:1–2:10)

Be a Bridge

GOD

Write in this space problems that preteens and their families face.

Write on the bridge a five letter word that helps us solve those problems.

WHY DID JOB SUFFER?

Where do you look for advice?

Do you ask others for advice? When you make decisions, how much importance do you place on advice you receive?

1. How often do you ask for advice?

_____ Always _____ Sometimes _____ Almost Never

2. How much are your decisions affected by the advice you receive?

A Little Bit   A lot

3. Who do you ask for Advice?

_____ Friends _____ Parents _____ Other Adults

4. How do you evaluate whether the advice is good or bad?

_____ Logic _____ Common Sense _____ Prayer

_____ The Bible _____ Experience

Friends?

???

ELIPHAZ: As I am the oldest and most respected, I will speak first. Job, you know that people reap what they sow. Can you mention a good person who has been punished by God? I have seen that many times sinners have lots of problems. Why don't you just confess your sin to God?

JOB: Eliphaz, your attitude disappoints me. I did not do anything wrong and I am not guilty of any sin. I believe that God is love. And although I do not understand what is happening, I know that my Redeemer lives.

BILDAD: Job, I think your attitude is incredible. Listen to me, God is just. I think your children died because they did something wrong. If you were really good, God would listen to your prayers.

JOB: Bildad, everything is in the hands of God. What I said is not because I do not respect God. I just think that there is another law that is operating in this situation.

ZOPHAR: I also think that you sinned. Otherwise, God would not have allowed this to happen to you. You must confess your sin and restore your relationship with God.

JOB: Zophar, it hurts me that you think I sinned. You declared me guilty without knowing exactly what happened.

ELIHU: God did not treat you as an enemy. He loves you. You should not question that. If good people suffer, it must be because they were about to do something bad. God is trying to get you away from sin. Repent while you have time.

40

Were Job's Friends Right?
Had Job Sinned?

Answer these questions:

1. What kind of advice did Job's friends give to him?

2. In what way were Job's friends kind to him?

3. How did Job's friends discourage him?

4. How did the friends react to Job's situation?

5. How did Job react to the advice of his friends?

6. Why did Job's friends not believe him?

7. What did Job do to deserve what had happened to him?

Read Job 33:9 and write Job's testimony.

Calamity or Consequece

Calamity: a great misfortune or disaster.

Consequence: the effect or result of something that previously happened.

When could lung cancer be a consequence?

When could it be a calamity?

When could it be a consequence to lose your job?

When could it be a calamity?

When could having AIDS be a consequence?

When could it be a calamity?

What is the most important thing that Job learned?

42

IMPORTANT DECISIONS I'VE MADE

Decisions I've Made	What helped me make this decision?
1.	1.
2.	2.
3.	3.
4.	4.
5.	5.
6.	6.
7.	7.
8.	8.
9.	9.
10.	10.

What did JOB think?

1. What did Job learn about God through suffering?

2. What does Job tell us in 42:1-2 about God?

3. How is Job's story similar to that of Jesus?

4. When good people suffer, do they always find an answer?

"I know that you can do all things.

What do I think?

1. What do you think is unfair in the world?

2. What do you think is unfair at school?

3. What do you think is unfair in your family?

4. What do you think is unfair about yourself?

5. Who is in control of all situations?

6. What can you do to fix them?

No plan of yours can be ruined." (Job 42:2 ICB)

What was the most important thing Job learned?

Love your enemies.

Go to church.

Share your belongings.

Be faithful in prayer.

Read good books.

Keep your mind pure.

Do to others what you want them to do to you.

Be careful what you say.

Read the Bible.

Respect the possessions of others.

Spend time with God.

Be slow to speak and quick to listen.

Tell the truth.

Trust in God.

Honor your parents.

Love your neighbor.

Be nice.

Put God first.

OBEYING GOD IS WORTH IT!

YOU BE THE JUDGE!

VERDICT

	JUST	UNJUST
Kristie's parents told her not to put on her new clothes to play in. One afternoon Sara invited her to the park. Kristie forgot to change her clothes and ruined her new pants. Kristie's mother made her stay home for a week.	☐	☐
Carl and Robert were throwing food during recess time. The principal was passing by, but he only saw Carl doing it, so he suspended Carl for a month.	☐	☐
Erica and her soccer team went out to eat after the game. Two of her teammates behaved very badly and embarrassed the coach. The coach said she wouldn't take the team out again for the rest of the season.	☐	☐

JOSHUA
THE LEADER

1. How did the first and second battles between Israel and Ai differ?

2. What does this story tell us about the consequences of disobeying God's commands?

3. What does this story tell us about the results of obeying God's commands?

4. Although Joshua was a great leader, what mistake did he make after the battle of Jericho?

5. What did Joshua do when he realized his mistake?

6. What happened as a result of the prayer of Joshua and the punishment of Achan?

CONSIDER AND ANSWER!

What are the consequences of disobeying God?

Follow Joshua's Example

Circle the words that describe Joshua.

Willing to ask for Forgiveness

Grumpy

Miracle Maker

Shy

Trustworthy

Obedient

Humble

Proud

Disobedient

Honest

Willing to Learn

What are the benefits of obeying God?

Why does God want us to obey him?

49

Medical Exam

Name: _____

My Pulse: *I feel that I obey God ____% of the time.*

My Blood Pressure:
- ❑ *High: I know I'm not obeying God.*
- ❑ *Low: I don't care if I obey God or not.*
- ❑ *Normal: I try to always obey God.*

Short-term Prognosis: *Today I need to:*
- ❑ *Thank God for His love and mercy.*
- ❑ *Ask God to forgive me for disobeying Him.*
- ❑ *Trust the God will help me to obey Him.*
- ❑ *Other* _____

Long-term Prognosis: *This week I'm going to...*

Lesson 14

THE AUTHORITY OF JESUS

Jesus went into the Temple. He threw out all the people who were buying and selling there. He turned over the tables that belonged to the men who were exchanging different kinds of money. And he turned over the benches of those who were selling doves. Jesus said to all the people there, "It is written in the Scriptures, 'My Temple will be a house where people will pray.' But you are changing God's house into a 'hideout for robbers.'"

(Matthew 21:12-13)

What authority did Jesus have?

Read Matthew 21:1-11.
1. In what way did Jesus demonstrate his authority in getting the donkey for the triumphal entry?
2. How did the crowd show their respect to Jesus when he arrived in Jerusalem?

Read Matthew 21:12-17.
1. In what way did Jesus demonstrate his authority to the money changers and sellers in the temple?
2. In what way did Jesus demonstrate his authority to the lame and the blind?
3. How did the Pharisees react when the children worshiped and praised Jesus?

Read Matthew 21:23-27.
1. How did Jesus react when the Pharisees questioned his authority?
2. How did the Pharisees react when Jesus questioned them?

Read Matthew 26:14-16; 28:16-20.
1. In what way did Judas ignore the authority of Jesus?
2. According to Matthew 28:18, what kind of authority did Jesus have?

"Then Jesus came to them and said, 'All authority in heaven and on earth has been given to me.'" (Matthew 28:18)

Who is the AUTHORITY?

What do you LOSE by obeying?

What do you GAIN by obeying?

Tim's parents asked him to go with them to visit his great-grandmother who lives in a nursing home. "I don't like going to that place. I've only seen her a couple of times and I don't really know her," he replied. "Besides, there's a game on T.V. today that I wanted to watch."

Luis and Bryan saw an old man with a cane walking down the street. "Let's go scare him and threaten to steal his cane!" Luis said. When Bryan said he didn't think they should, Luis replied, "There's nothing wrong with that. We won't hurt him, just scare him a little."

At school, Rita saw a little girl drop some money out of her pocket. Since no one had seen what happened, she picked up the money and put it in her pocket. An inner voice told her, "Return that money to the little girl."

For many months Phil worked and saved money to buy a new bicycle. At last he had the money he needed. In his devotional he read Malachi 3:10, which talks about tithing. But he had never tithed. "If I give my tithe, I can't buy the bicycle now and I'll have to wait several more weeks," Phil thought.

Brenda was riding her bicycle home and decided to take a shortcut. Suddenly, she came to a sign that said "Bridge Closed". Brenda thought, "That sign is only for cars. I can cross the bridge with my bicycle."

WHO IS HE...

to your friends?

to you?

I AM

the resurrection and the life. The one who believes in me will live, even though they die; and whoever lives by believing in me will never die.
(John 11:25-26)

What do you lose by obeying Jesus?

What do you gain by obeying Jesus?

PRAYER: THE SOURCE OF POWER

Jesus Prayed

READ **Luke 22:39-46**
What do these verses reveal about Jesus' attitude towards his death?

Why did he insist that his disciples needed to pray?

READ **Luke 22:47-53; and Matthew 26:55-56**
How did the disciples react when they arrested Jesus?

Could the situation have been different if the disciples had prayed?

READ **Luke 22:54-62**
Why did Peter deny knowing Jesus?

How did Peter act wrong?

A SOURCE OF POWER

Psalm 25:11
Jeremiah 29:12
Jeremiah 42:3
Matthew 5:44
Luke 6:28
Luke 22:40
James 5:13-14

Look for these Bible verses. What do they tell you about the importance of prayer? How do these verses apply to your life?

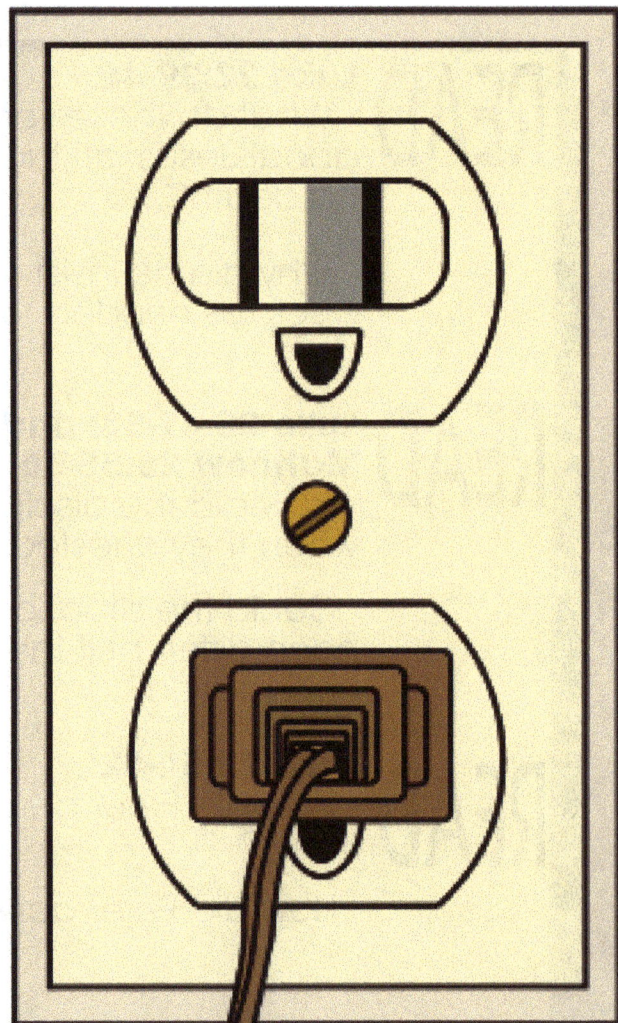

Which one do you use?

Praise

Intercession

Confession

Meditation

Petition

Thanksgiving

Read each sentence and decide which type of prayer it plugs into.

Lord, please forgive me for treating my brother badly.

God, please help my friend because his family has problems.

Lord, please help me do what it says in Proverbs 3:5; Trust in the Lord with all your heart, and lean not on your own understanding.

God, you are wonderful. You are the Creator of all that exists, and that is why I worship you.

Lord, you helped me when those young people wanted to mistreat me. Thank you for giving me the strength to be calm and stay away from trouble.

God, I ask you to help me in my exam. I studied a lot and I am sure that with your help everything will be fine.

My Source of Power and Strength

My Prayer List

Sunday

Monday

Tuesday

Wednesday

Thursday

Friday

Saturday

Answers to Prayers

58

JESUS' TRIAL

Have you ever gone to trial?

JESUS'

Part 1: Judgment by Annas and Caiaphas

Characters: Narrator, Jesus, Annas, Caiaphas, witnesses, chief priest, Sanhedrin.

Narrator: Jesus was arrested in the garden of Gethsemane, where he had been praying. The soldiers took him to Annas, the ex-high priest, who was the father-in-law of Caiaphas, the new high priest.

Annas: Who are those men who follow you? What lies did you tell them so that they would believe in you?

Jesus: I spoke openly and always taught in the synagogues or at the temple. I didn't say anything in secret. Why are you asking me? Wouldn't it be better ask those who heard me?

Chief Priest: (Hitting Jesus) Is that the way you answer the high priest?

Jesus: If I said something wrong, tell me, but if I told the truth, why did you hit me?

Narrator: After listening to him, Annas sent him tied up to Caiaphas.

In the house of Caiphas, the Sanhedrin were assembled. These leaders sought to find any evidence against Jesus. Many wanted to sentence him to death. The problem was there was no reason to kill him, although false witnesses had told lies about him.

Witnesses: This man said, "I will tear down this temple made by hand, and in three days I will build another not made by hand."

Caiaphas: Do you have something to say?

Narrator: Jesus was silent.

Caiaphas: Are you the Messiah, the Son of the Blessed One?

Jesus: I am. And you will see the Son of Man sitting at the right hand of the Mighty One and coming on the clouds of heaven.

Caiaphas: (Tearing his robe) Blasphemy! We do not need any more witnesses. You yourselves have heard the blasphemy. What do you think?

Chief Priest: He's guilty! The punishment must be death!

Narrator: Then they began to spit on Jesus' face and hit him with their fists.

Chief Priest: Tell us, who hit you? Show us that you are the Messiah and tell us who hit you.

Part 2: Trial before Pilate

Characters: Narrator, Pilate, Jesus, temple officials, crowd.

Narrator: It was very early in the morning when they took Jesus before Pilate.

Pilate: What are you accusing this man of?

Chief Priest: He is guilty. We would not have brought him before you if we were not sure that he is a criminal.

Pilate: Then judge him by your own laws.

Chief Priest: We can not sentence him to death, but it is the punishment he deserves for his crimes. He is destroying our nation, and betraying Rome because he incites the people not to pay their

60

TRIAL

taxes to Caesar. In addition, he claims to be the Christ, the king of the Jews.

Narrator: Meanwhile, Jesus remained silent.

Pilate: Are you the King of the Jews?

Jesus: Is that what you think or did others tell you about me?

Pilate: Your people and chief priests delivered you to me. What did you do?

Jesus: My kingdom is not of this world; if it were my servants would fight to prevent my arrest by the Jewish leaders; But my kingdom is not from here.

Pilate: So, are you king?

Jesus: You say I'm a king. For this I was born and for this I have come to the world to testify to the truth. Everyone on the side of truth listens to me.

Pilate: What is the truth? (Pilate leaves to talk to the Jews) I find no basis for a charge against him.

Narrator: It was customary for a prisoner to be released at the time of Passover.

Pilate: Do you want me to free the King of the Jews?

Crowd: No, not him! We want Barabbas!

Narrator: Barabbas was imprisoned for inciting a rebellion in the city, and for murder.

Pilate: Whip Jesus! Maybe with that they remain calm.

Narrator: The soldiers, obeying Pilate's order, whipped Jesus until blood spilled from his back. Some soldiers made a crown of thorns and put it on Jesus.

Pilate: Jesus is innocent. I do not find any fault in him.

Crowd: Crucify him! Crucify him!

Pilate: You take him and crucify him, because I find no basis for a charge against him.

Chief Priests: We have a law, and according to that law he must die because he claimed to be the Son of God.

Pilate: (Addressing Jesus) Where are you from? Do you refuse to talk to me? Do you not realize that I have the power to set you free or to crucify you?

Narrator: Pilate was looking for a way to set him free.

Jesus: You would have no authority over me if it were not given to you from above.

Chief Priests: If you let this man go, you are no friend of Caesar. Anyone who claims to be a king opposes Caesar.

Pilate: Here you have your King!

Crowd: We do not want him! Crucify him!

Pilate: Shall I crucify your King?

Chief Priest: We have no king but Caesar.

Narrator: Then Pilate handed Jesus over to them to be crucified.

(Mark 14:58 - 65; John 18:19 – 19:16)

61

Will You Stand Firm?

"Blessed is the one who perseveres under trial because, having stood the test, that person will receive the crown of life that the Lord has promised to those who love him." (James 1:12)

JESUS' DEATH

What Would You Sacrifice for Your Sins?

In Old Testament times, people offered sacrifices to express gratitude to God or to ask for forgiveness. The first animal sacrifice was to cover the sin of Adam and Eve. Although the people in the Old Testament also brought grain offerings, it was common to sacrifice an animal.

The prophets warned the people that sacrifices were not enough if they did not love and obey God. The sacrifices of the Old Testament announced the way in which Jesus would die.

John writes in the New Testament. "My dear children, I write this to you so that you will not sin. But if anybody does sin, we have an advocate with the Father—Jesus Christ, the Righteous One. He is the atoning sacrifice for our sins, and not only for ours but also for the sins of the whole world." (1 John 2:1-2)

Why did Jesus have to die?

Read the verses and fill in the missing words.

1. Who sinned? Adam and Eve sinned, and changed the original relationship between mankind and God. Sin separated all of humanity from God. God is love and there is no sin in him.

"For _____ have _____, and fall short of the glory of God."

(Romans 3:23)

2. What are the consequences of sin?

"For the wages of sin is _____, but the _____ of God is _____ _____ in Christ Jesus, our Lord."

(Romans 6:23)

WHAT DOES THE DEATH

Look at the pictures and compare the way people approached God in the Old Testament and how we can approach God now.

64

3. Can mankind get rid of sin? God has tried to restore his relationship with people. In Bible times, people offered sacrifices, but often they did not change their attitudes. Others tried to fix the relationship by doing good deeds. But none of those methods were enough.

For it is by _____ you have been saved, through _____ – and this is not from yourselves, it is the _____ of God – not by _____, so that no one can _____."

(Ephesians 2:8-9)

4. How can we solve the problem of sin?

"For God so _____ the world that he gave his _____ and only _____, that _____ believes in him shall not _____ but have _____ _____." (John 3:16)

"If we _____ our sins, he is _____ and just and will _____ us our sins and _____ us from all unrighteousness."

(1 John 1:9)

5. How did Jesus help us restore our relationship with God? From the moment we believe that Jesus is the Son of God and we ask forgiveness for our sins, our relationship with God is restored.

"Yet to all who did _____ him, to those who _____ in his _____, he gave the right to become _____ of God."

(John 1:12)

OF JESUS MEAN TO ME?

GAME OF MEMORY

Solve the Puzzle

I	am	het	ruce nrei orts	N ad	eht	l f.	HET
eon	hwO	sbveiele	Ni	e m	ILWL	Eliv,	eenv
uthhgo	th y	eid;	dan	rveheow	il sev	yb	bve iei Ing
		em	LLIW	renve	die.		
		JOHN	1:	2⁵ — ²6			

JESUS LIVES !

HE LIVES!

The angel said to the women, "Do not be afraid, for I know that you are looking for Jesus, who was crucified. He is not here; he has risen, just as he said. Come and see the place where he lay. Then go quickly and tell his disciples, 'He has risen from the dead and is going ahead of you into Galilee. There you will see him.' Now I have told you."
(Matthew 28:5-7)

SCENE 1:

IN THE TOMB
CHARACTERS: NARRATOR, ANGEL, TWO WOMEN, JESUS.

Narrator: At dawn on the first day of the week, Mary Magdalene and the other Mary went to the tomb. As they were walking, the earth began to tremble and there was a great earthquake.
Then an angel came down from heaven, rolled the stone away and sat on it. His appearance was like lightning, and his clothes were as white as snow. Upon seeing him, the guards began to tremble and they became like dead men.
Angel: (Talking to the women) Do not be afraid; I know that you are looking for Jesus, the one who was crucified. He is not here, he has risen. Come and see the place where he lay. (The two women look inside the tomb.)
Now go and tell the disciples, "He has risen from the dead and is going ahead of you into Galilee. There you will see him."
Narrator: The women, full of joy, ran to give the good news to the disciples. Suddenly they saw someone.
Jesus: Greetings!
Narrator: The two women knelt to worship him.
Jesus: Do not be afraid. Go and tell my brothers to go to Galilee. There you will see me.
(Matthew 28:1-8)

SCENE 2:

CHARACTERS: NARRATOR, CHIEF PRIESTS, GUARDS. THE GUARDS TALK TO THE PRIESTS.

Narrator: Some of the guards went to tell the priests what had happened.
Chief Priests: (They talk to each other and then give a bag of coins to each guard.) Listen well. Tell everyone that the disciples came during the night and stole the body of Jesus while you were sleeping. Don't worry; we know that you could be killed if you had fallen asleep while on duty, but we will protect you.
Narrator: The guards took the money and said everything as the Chief Priests had indicated. The story that the disciples stole the body of Jesus still circulates among the Jews.

(Matthew 28:11-15)

SCENE 3:

CHARACTERS: NARRATOR, 11 DISCIPLES, JESUS. JESUS SPEAKS WITH HIS DISCIPLES

Narrator: The eleven disciples went to Galilee, to the mountain where Jesus told them they would find him. When they saw him, they fell to their knees to worship him. However, some still doubted that it was really Jesus.
Jesus: "All authority in heaven and on earth has been given to me. Therefore go and make disciples of all nations, baptizing them in the name of the Father and of the Son and of the Holy Spirit, teaching them to obey everything I have commanded you. And surely I am with you always, to the very end of the age."
(Matthew 28:16-20)

Lesson 19

GOD IS IN CONTROL

God did it!

1. The friend Jesus resurrected (John 11:43-44).
2. Mount where the fire of God consumed a wet sacrifice (1 Kings 18:19, 36-38).
3. Appearance of the army with horses and chariots of fire that protected Elisha and his servant (2 Kings 6:15-17).
4. Prophet that God used to resurrect the son of a widow (1 Kings 17:22).
5. Sea that was opened for the people of God to escape from the Egyptian army (Exodus 14:21-22; 15:4).
6. What Peter and John did in the name of Jesus to help a lame man (Acts 3:1-7).
7. One of the foods that Jesus multiplied to feed five thousand people (Mark 6:41).
8. The one who resurrected Jesus (Acts 2:32).
9. River that stopped flowing for Joshua and the Israelites to pass (Joshua 3:15-16).

Solve the alphabet soup using the 9 key answers.

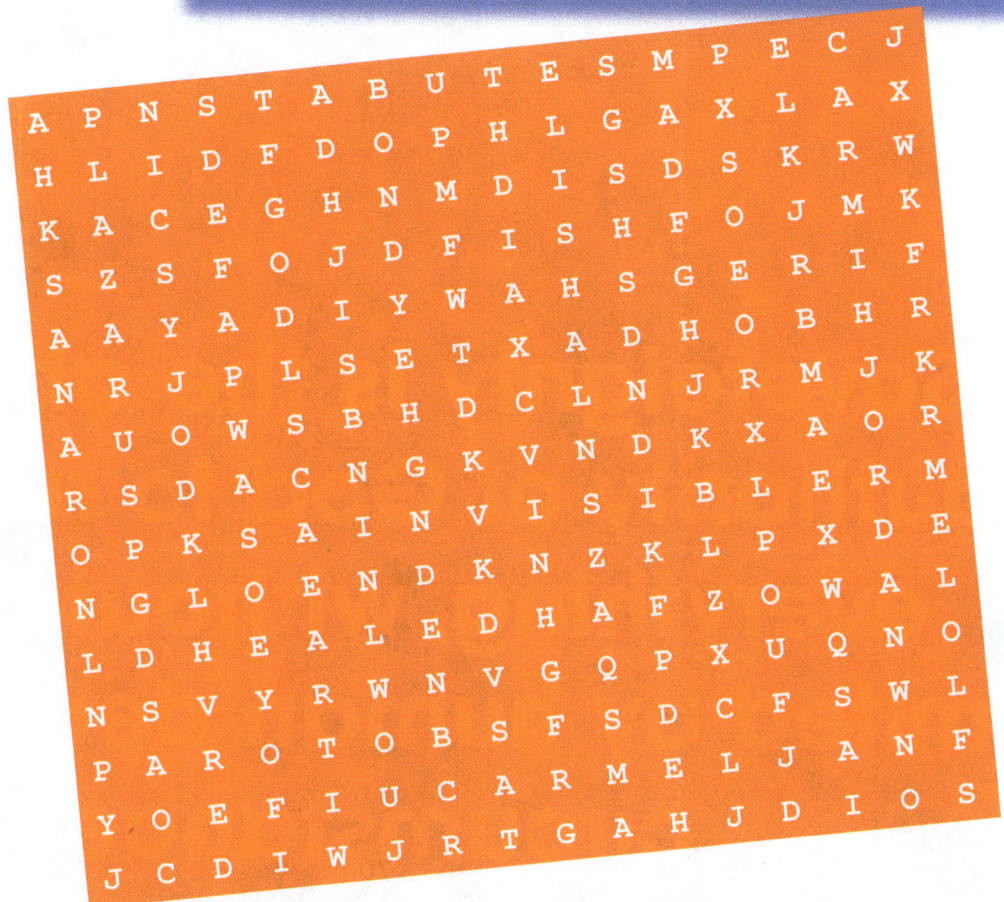

```
A P N S T A B U T E S M P E C J
H L I D F D O P H L G A X L A X
K A C E G H N M D I S D S K R W
S Z S F O J D F I S H F O J M K
A A Y A D I Y W A H S G E R I F
N R J P L S E T X A D H O B H R
A U O W S B H D C L N J R M J K
R S D A C N G K V N D K X A O R
O P K S A I N V I S I B L E R M
N G L O E N D K N Z K L P X D E
L D H E A L E D H A F Z O W A L
N S V Y R W N V G Q P X U Q N O
P A R O T O B S F S D C F S W L
Y O E F I U C A R M E L J A N F
J C D I W J R T G A H J D I O S
```

God showed his

SOVEREIGNTY

over

THE EVENTS (battle)
NATURE (hail)
WEATHER (the sun)

Sovereignty is the absolute authority of God to rule over everything, without being limited by human decisions or circumstances.

70

A M A Z I N G

Our help in the midst of problems

1. Why did Joshua help the people of Gibeon?

2. Why did God send hail?

3. In your opinion, why doesn't God always work miracles to fulfill his plans?

Our Amazing God

1. What does the word "sovereignty" mean to you?

2. How does the sovereignty of God help us?

3. Sometimes we call kings and queens "sovereigns" because they have control over their country. God is sovereign. What should our relationship with him be like?

How Do You Feel?

Circle the words that express how you feel knowing that our sovereign God can work miracles.

Joy

ashamed

Astonished

Sad

Enthusiastic

Stressed

Confused

Afraid

Proud

"...for the Lord your God has given them into your hand."

(Joshua 10:19*b*)

A GOOD START FOR SAMSON

What do you THINK?

Agree   Disagree

○ ○ **1.** As a Christian, I am free to do whatever I want.

○ ○ **2.** As a Christian, I must ask for forgiveness if I sin.

○ ○ **3.** God does not care how I live.

○ ○ **4.** The Bible has such high demands that people find it difficult to fulfill them.

○ ○ **5.** Through the Holy Spirit, God empowers us to live in holiness.

○ ○ **6.** God wants us to live in holiness.

Samson

The neighboring peoples of the Israelites worshiped false gods. Many Israelite children, when they grew up, wanted to imitate them. They made images, put them in their courtyards and bowed before them to worship them.

As people turned away from God, he allowed them to have problems. In the coastal area lived the Philistines, who were cruel and strong. For 40 years they dominated the tribes of Israel that lived nearby. The Philistines worshiped the god Dagon. This idol had a man's face and hands, and the body of a fish. The Philistines built a great temple for Dagon in their capital city.

However, not all Israelites worshiped false gods. Some loved and served God. Among them was Manoah and his wife, an elderly couple who had no children.

One day, an angel told Manoah's wife: "You are barren and childless, but you are going to become pregnant and give birth to a son. Now see to it that you drink no wine or other fermented drink and that you do not eat anything unclean. You will become pregnant and have a son whose head is never to be touched by a razor because the boy is to be a Nazirite, dedicated to God from the womb. He will take the lead in delivering Israel from the hands of the Philistines."

When she told Manoah about this, he prayed: "Pardon your servant, Lord. I beg you to let the man of God you sent to us come again to teach us how to bring up the boy who is to be born."

God heard Manoah and when his wife was out in the field, the angel returned, so she ran to call her husband. Manoah asked the angel, "When your words are fulfilled, what is to be the rule that governs the boy's life and work?"

The angel replied, "Your wife must do all that I have told her."

Then Manoah and his wife offered a sacrifice to God. When the flame ascended from the altar to heaven, Manoah and his wife saw the angel of the Lord rise in the flame.

After a while, Manoah's wife gave birth to a son and named him Samson. His parents raised him according to the Nazirite vows. They never cut his hair; they did not allow him to eat unclean food or drink any kind of wine. These were some of the restrictions that the Nazirites had to fulfill. Samson grew strong and God blessed him. (Judges 13:2-24)

The New Testament tells us about another Nazirite man.

Zechariah had left his home in the mountains to fulfill his time of service as a priest in the temple. Since there were many priests, they took turns ministering.

Zechariah and his wife Elizabeth loved and served God, and awaited the coming of the Messiah, but they had no children.

Twice a day Zechariah would take burning coals from the altar and take them to the sanctuary to offer incense to God. One day, when entering the sanctuary, Zechariah saw an angel and was afraid.

and John

The angel said to him, "Do not be afraid, Zechariah; your prayer has been heard. Your wife Elizabeth will bear you a son, and you are to call him John. He will be a joy and delight to you, and many will rejoice because of his birth, for he will be great in the sight of the Lord. He is never to drink wine or other fermented drink, and he will be filled with the Holy Spirit even before he is born. He will bring back many of the people of Israel to the Lord their God. And he will go on before the Lord, in the spirit and power of Elijah, to turn the hearts of the parents to their children and the disobedient to the wisdom of the righteous—to make ready a people prepared for the Lord."

It seemed incredible to Zechariah what the angel was saying, so he asked, "How will I know this? Because I am old and my wife is old."

The angel replied, "I am Gabriel. I stand in the presence of God, and I have been sent to speak to you and to tell you this good news. And now you will be silent and not able to speak until the day this happens, because you did not believe my words."

Those who were in the courtyard of the temple wondered why Zechariah took so long in the sanctuary. When at last he came out, he could not speak. He communicated by making signs. Then they realized that he had seen a vision. When he completed his ministry, he went home. Later, his wife Elizabeth conceived and gave birth to a boy.

According to Jewish custom, the father named his son eight days after birth. That day, relatives and friends arrived, hoping that the boy would be given his father's name.

When Elizabeth announced that the baby would be called John, they all looked at Zechariah to see his reaction. But he wrote on a tablet: "His name is John."

Immediately he regained his speech and praised God. Then, he prophesied that his son would go before the Lord to prepare the way. John would teach the people that they could be saved if they repented of their sins.

He grew big and strong. And when he was almost 30 years old, he left home and began to preach next to the Jordan River. People from all over came to hear him, and he baptized those who repented of their sins. One day, John had the privilege of baptizing Jesus. Because he baptized people, they called him John the Baptist. (Luke 1:13-24, 57)

How were these men alike?

How were they different?

75

Dear Me:

I try to live a Holy life.
Sometimes ...

"But just as he who called you is holy, so be holy in all you do."

(1 Peter 1:15)

"I can do all this through him who gives me strength."

(Philippians 4:13)

A VERY STRONG MAN

Privileges and responsibility go together. If you want your parents or teachers to give you privileges, you have to show that you are responsible. Write in the acrostic ways you can show that you are responsible.

I CAN BE . . .

Respect my parents' decisions.

E

S

P

O

N

S

I

B

L

E

The Road of Revenge

1. What was Samson's first mistake?

2. Why do you think Samson's parents didn't want him to marry a Philistine woman?

3. How did Samson show his amazing strength?

4. Where did Samson get the idea for a riddle?

5. What did Samson do to pay those who answered the riddle?

6. Why did Samson catch foxes and tie lit torches to their tails?

7. What did the Philistines do after Samson burned their crops?

8. What did Samson do to the Philistines who wanted to trap him?

9. What did God do with Samson after he destroyed the Philistines?

10. What does this story tell us about God's relationship with Samson?

Where does this road end?

SAMSON

STRENGTHS

_____
_____
_____
_____
_____
_____

WEAKNESSES

_____
_____
_____
_____
_____
_____

A different ending to the story

Starting from the day that Samson wanted a Philistine wife, write what his story might have been like if he had made good decisions.

Good Relationships

? What does God expect from me regarding my relationship with him

?

? What can I expect from God in regard to my relationship with him **?**

What happened to Samson?

Narrator: Samson fell in love with a woman named Delilah. The Philistine rulers visited her to propose a deal.

Philistines: Try to deceive him to find out the secret of his strength. That way we can defeat him. If you do, each one of us will give you one thousand one hundred silver shekels.

Narrator: Delilah wanted the money, so she tried to get Samson to tell her his secret.

Delilah: Tell me the secret of your strength and how you can be tied up and subdued.

Samson: If anyone ties me with seven fresh bowstrings that have not been dried, I'll become as weak as any other man.

Narrator: The Philistine rulers brought her seven fresh bowstrings that had not been dried, and Delilah tied up Samson while some Philistines waited in hiding.

Delilah: Samson, the Philistines are here to attack you!

Narrator: Samson got up, breaking the bowstrings easily. Delilah was disappointed to see that Samson had not told her the truth. So, she asked again what his secret was.

Delilah: You have made a fool of me; you lied to me. Come now, tell me how you can be tied.

Samson: If you tie me tightly with new ropes that no one has used, then I will become as weak as any other man.

Narrator: Delilah tied Samson with new ropes and, like the first time, the Philistines were hiding in the next room.

Delilah: Samson, the Philistines are here to attack you!

Narrator: Samson broke the ropes as if they had been threads.

Delilah: You made a fool of me again! You have to tell me how to tie you up.

Samson: If you weave the seven braids of my hair into the fabric on the loom and tighten it with the pin, I'll become as weak as any other man.

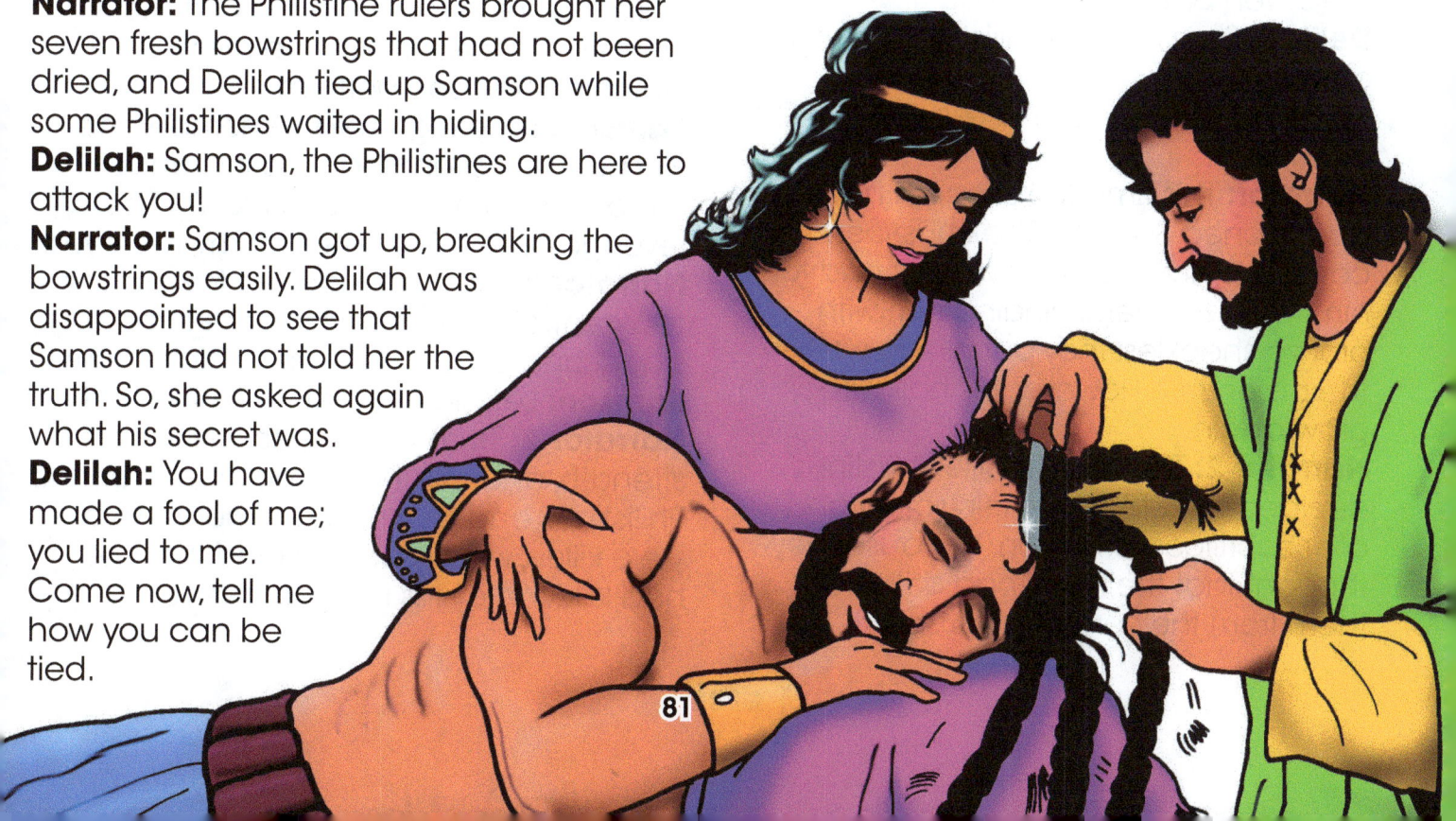

81

Narrator: While Samson was sleeping, Delilah did everything he had said.

Delilah: Samson, the Philistines are here to attack you!

Narrator: Samson instantly got up and pulled up the pin and the loom with the fabric.

Delilah: Liar! How can you say you love me? You have made of fool of me three times, and you still won't tell me the secret of your strength.

Narrator: Delilah kept insisting, asking the same question over and over. Finally, Samson got tired of her nagging and told her his secret.

Samson: No one has ever cut my hair, because before I was born I was consecrated to God as a Nazirite. If you cut my hair, I will lose my strength and be as weak as any man.

Narrator: Delilah realized that this time he had told her the truth. Then she sent word to the Philistine rulers: "Come back once more; he has told me everything!" They arrived with the money in their hands. After Delilah put Samson to sleep on her lap, she called a man to come and cut off the seven braids of his head.

Delilah: Samson, the Philistines are here to attack you!

Samson: (Waking up) I'll escape just like I did before.

Narrator: This time the strength had abandoned Samson. The Philistines captured him, took his eyes out and took him to Gaza. There, binding him with bronze shackles, they put him to work in the prison mill. However, his hair began to grow again.

Narrator 2: The rulers of the Philistines decided to celebrate their victory and offer sacrifices to Dagon, because they thought that their god had delivered them from their enemy, Samson.

In the middle of the celebration, they asked for Samson to be brought out to entertain them. Then they stood him among the pillars. Samson said to the young man who was guiding him:

Samson: Put me where I can feel the pillars that support the temple, so I may lean against them.

Narrator 2: The temple was full of men and women, and all the rulers of the Philistines were there. On the roof there were about three thousand people watching Samson perform.

Samson: Sovereign Lord, remember me. Please, God, strengthen me just once more, and let me with one blow get revenge on the Philistines for my two eyes.

Narrator 2: Samson reached toward the two central pillars on which the temple stood, and braced himself against them.

Samson: Let me die with the Philistines!

Narrator 2: Then he pushed with all his strength, and the temple collapsed on the Philistines and all who were there. More were killed when Samson died than he had killed in all his life. (Judges 16)

6. In your opinion, why did Samson's life end the way it did?

5. What do you think God wanted for Samson's life?

4. What should have been some hints to Samson that he couldn't trust Delilah?

3. What was the result of Samson revealing his secret to Delilah?

2. What could Samson have done to avoid his fall?

1. When did the fall of Samson begin?

DECISIONS

Trust in the Lord with all your heart

and lean not on your own understanding;

In all your ways submit to him,

and he will make your paths straight.

(Proverbs 3:5-6)

_____

has memorized:

Philippians 4:13

John 11:25-26

Proverbs 3:5-6

Lesson 23

OUR GREAT CREATOR

What a LIFE!

The trees are part of God's creation.

In your opinion, why did God create the trees?

Why are trees so important to creation?

In your opinion, why did God create so many trees?

What can we learn from God through the trees he created?

85

Follow the Clues

DEBATE CLUB
Meeting
Mon. 4:30

TIGRES

In what ways can someone tell you
what kind of person this boy is?

FIND
ANSWERS
TO YOUR
QUESTIONS

CREATE

Ps.	51:10	**C** in me a pure heart, O God, and renew a steadfast spirit within me.
Mal.	2:10	Did not one God **C** us?
Eph.	2:15	to **C** in himself

CREATED

Gen.	1:1	In the beginning God **C** the heavens and the earth.
Gen.	1:27	in the image of God he **C**.
Gen.	1:27	male and female he **C** them.
Mark	13:19	when God **C** the world
Col.	1:16	For in him all things were **C**
1 Ti.	4:4	For everything God **C** is good.
Rev.	10:6	who **C** the heavens

CREATION

Ps.	96:13	Let all **C** rejoice before the Lord.
Mark	10:6	beginning of **C** God 'made them male and female
Rom.	1:20	For since the **C** of the world.
2 Cor.	5:17	the new **C** has come:
Col.	1:15	the firstborn over all **C**.

CREATOR

Gen.	14:19	**C** of heaven and earth.
Ecc.	12:1	Remember your **C**
1 Pet.	4:19	commit themselves to their faithful **C**

Next to each sentence write the reference to a verse that has the same idea:

1. God created the world. _____

2. Everything God created is good. _____

3. God created us in his image. _____

4. If anyone is in Christ, the new creation has come. _____

5. Remember your Creator while you are young. _____

6. Since the creation of the world, the invisible qualities of God have been clearly seen. _____

What does creation teach you about:

1. who God is?

2. the order of God?

3. his love for beauty?

4. his imagination & creativity?

5. his care for people?

6. his power and authority?

IT'S NO ACCIDENT

THE SAME
or
different?

Biblical Statements:

"The earth was formless and empty, darkness was over the surface of the deep." (Genesis 1: 2)

"And God said: 'Let there be light.'" (Genesis 1: 3)

"And God said, 'Let there be a vault between the waters to separate water from water.' So God made the vault and separated the water under the vault from the water above it. And it was so. God called the vault 'sky'." (Genesis 1: 6-8a)

"Then God said, 'Let the land produce vegetation: seed-bearing plants and trees on the land that bear fruit with seeds in it, according to their various kinds" (Genesis 1:11),

"And God said, 'Let there be lights in the vault of the sky to separate the day from the night, and let them serve as signs to mark sacred times, and days and years, and let them be lights in the vault of the sky to give light on the earth'" (Genesis 1: 14-15).

"And God said, 'Let the water teem with living creatures, and let birds fly above the earth across the vault of the sky'" (Genesis 1:20).

"And God said, 'Let the land produce living creatures according to their kinds: the livestock, the creatures that move along the ground, and the wild animals, each according to its kind'" (Genesis 1:24).

"So God created mankind in his own image, in the image of God he created them; male and female he created them" (Genesis 1:27).

Scientific statements:

A common belief is that a "divine being" made all living beings. Since those events would be supernatural, they can not be proven scientifically; that is, we can not repeat them, control them or detect them with our senses.

There are two main hypotheses about the origin of life. One states that millions of years ago the atmosphere of the earth was very different from how it is today. Instead of being formed by oxygen and nitrogen, it is thought to have large amounts of carbon dioxide, water vapor, ammonia and methane. Perhaps the sun's rays caused these substances to combine, forming compound chemicals such as proteins. For thousands of years, these compounds grouped together, forming cells that could continue the processes of life.

The second hypothesis is that life on earth originated from meteorites, since some of these chemicals that produce proteins have been found in meteorites that have been discovered on earth.

In the past, before human beings and even dinosaurs walked the earth, there was only life in the ancient seas.

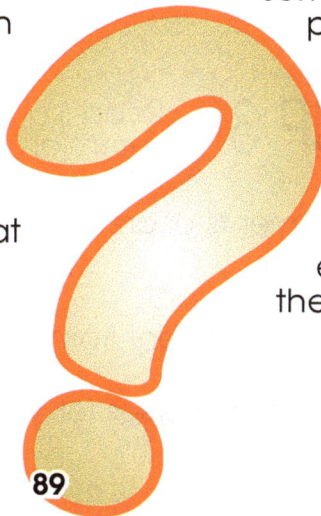

Questions about Creation

GROUP 1   Read Job 38:1-11

1. What elements of creation do these verses mention?

2. What does it mean when God says that he laid the earth's foundation, marked off its dimensions and laid its cornerstone?

3. How do you think Job felt after God asked him these questions?

4. What do these verses tell you about God?

GROUP 2   Read Psalm 95:3-5; 102:25-27

1. What elements of creation do these verses mention?

2. What feelings or emotions are expressed in these two passages?

3. What do these verses tell you about God?

GROUP 3   Read Isaiah 48:12-13; Jeremiah 10:11-13

1. What elements of creation do these verses mention?

2. How is God different from false idols or gods?

3. What do these verses tell you about God?

Which of these phrases represent a scientific point of view?

- God had nothing to do with creation.

- The first forms of life existed in the ocean.

- Water is composed of two molecules of hydrogen and one molecule of oxygen H_2O.

- God does not exist.

- Humans arrived on earth after animals.

CAN YOU EXPLAIN...

... how televisions receive signals and transform them into images and sounds?

Does that prevent you from watching television?

... how ingredients mixed together result in a delicious dessert?

Does that prevent you from eating dessert?

... how God created the heavens and the earth?

Does that prevent you from believing that God created you?

"NO" TO REJECTION!

1. What makes people feel like they are worthless?

2. What do many people base their worth on?

What is the image of God?

The word "image", commonly understood to mean a likeness of a person or thing to another, or a reflection or representation of such, appears numerous times in the Bible.

The divine image in man is not physical, for God is a Spirit without physical form. But He has shared that very spiritual nature with mankind. It is that quality which makes mankind unique among and superior to all other earthly creatures, giving him the ability to commune and fellowship with his Creator.

People have intellectual ability; that is, we can know, reason, imagine, remember, judge and make decisions freely.

We can reflect the moral image of God. Because of sin mankind lost its original holiness, but we can choose to ask for forgiveness and restore that relationship with God. As a Christian grows and matures, he/she better reflects the likeness of God.

Today the word "image" is often used when referring to someone's reputation. "Having a good image" of a person means to be well thought of. This can prompt Christians to be aware of the impression that their appearance and behavior have on others.

(Paraphrased from R. S. Taylor, J. K. Grider and W. H. Taylor; Beacon Dictionary of Theology, Beacon Hill Press of Kansas City, Kansas City, Missouri, 1983, pp. 272).

Underline the sentences in the paragraph above that answer the following questions:

1. Does God have a body like a human being?

2. How are people different from animals?

3. How can you reflect the image of God?

SIN'S TRAP

Why is it so bad to eat fruit?

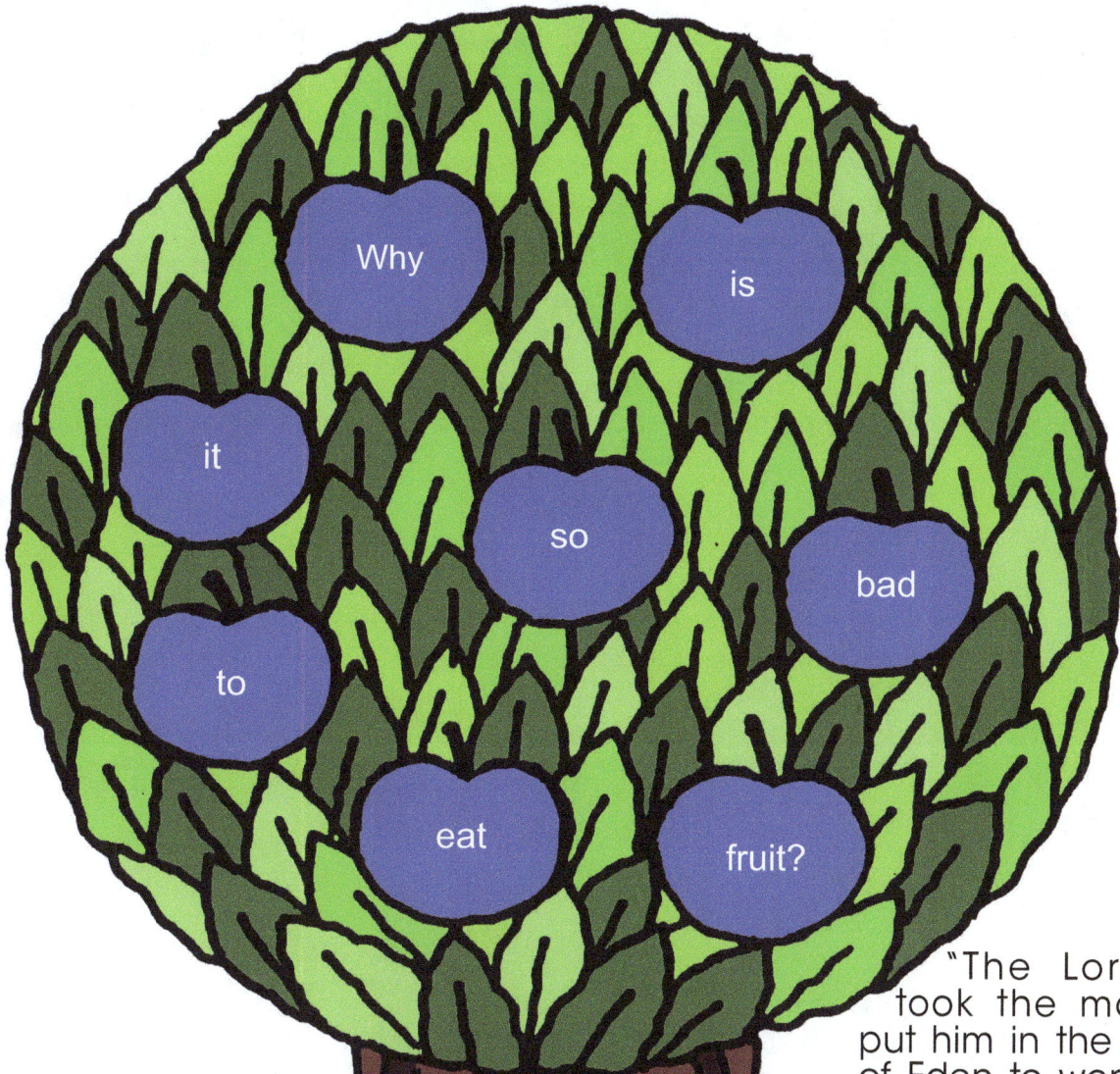

"The Lord God took the man and put him in the Garden of Eden to work it and take care of it. And the Lord God commanded the man, "You are free to eat from any tree in the garden; but you must not eat from the tree of the knowledge of good and evil, for when you eat from it you will certainly die."

(Genesis 2:15-17)

TEMPTATION TRAP

Will Rodger be able to cross the field of temptation without problems?

Read the verses to see what temptations Adam and Eve faced.

How do preteens face those temptations today?

Is it true that God said that? (Genesis 3:1)

God didn't tell them the truth. (Genesis 3:4)

God doesn't want them to receive something good. (Genesis 3:5)

It looks yummy! It can't be bad if it seems so good. (Genesis 3:6)

Convince someone else to do it too! (Genesis 3:6)

DANGER! OPEN PITS!

What can you do to resist TEMPTATION?

_____
_____
_____
_____
_____

How does God help us when we are tempted?

Write an A if you agree with the phrase.
Write a D if you disagree.

_____ The Holy Spirit helps us know if an action is right or wrong.

_____ Once a Christian decides to resist temptation, God will give him/her the strength to stay firm.

_____ God may intervene through a miracle to ward off temptation.

_____ If God does not take away the temptation, then it is our fault if we fall.

_____ When facing a temptation, God can help us remember appropriate Bible verses.

_____ God will provide a way to escape from temptation, but we must find the escape route and use it.

WHAT HAPPENS IF YOU FAIL?

How can you restore your relationship with God?

■ **WE HAVE ALL DISOBEYED GOD.**

"For all have sinned and fall short of the glory of God."

(Romans 3:23)

■ **THE ONLY WAY TO BE FORGIVEN IS BY HAVING FAITH, TRUSTING IN GOD.**

"For it is by grace you have been saved, through faith— and this is not from yourselves, it is the gift of God— not by works, so that no one can boast."

(Ephesians 2:8-9)

■ **GOD WILL FORGIVE YOU FOR THE BAD THINGS YOU HAVE DONE IF YOU CONFESS IT.**

"If we confess our sins, he is faithful and just and will forgive us our sins and purify us from all unrighteousness."

(1 John 1:9)

■ **CONFESSING OUR SINS MEANS:**

1. Admit that you have disobeyed God (sinned).
2. Repent (be sorry) of your sins.
3. Be willing to stop disobeying God.
4. Ask God to forgive you.

■ **GOD HAS PROMISED THAT IF YOU CONFESS YOUR SINS AND FOLLOW HIM, YOU CAN BE HIS CHILD.**

"Yet to all who did receive him, to those who believed in his name, he gave the right to become children of God."

(John 1:12)

98

Lesson 27

GOD GAVE US A MISSION

REPORT FROM SPACE

1. What are some amazing features of the earth that you've seen?

2. How are the inhabitants of the earth using their world?

3. How are the inhabitants of the earth taking care of their world?

THE RESPONSIBILITY GOD HAS GIVEN MANKIND

God gave people the ability and power to govern other living things that inhabit the earth. God gave people that privilege; but people must give an account of the way they use that privilege. This responsibility does not include the right to abuse animals.

God also gave people the right to use the fruit of plants and trees to produce food, but without destroying creation. Proper care of plant life includes the use and conservation of natural resources.

Animals also depend on plants to survive. So, people have the responsibility to take care of creation, supply their needs and at the same time, conserve the natural life cycle of plants and animals.

Use your Bible and the above information to answer the following questions:

1 What responsibility did God give to mankind? (Genesis 1:26-28; 2:15; Psalm 8:6-8).

2 In what way does sin affect the way mankind takes care of God's creation? (Genesis 2:17-19).

3 Why do you think God asked us to be responsible for his creation?

These animals are **EXHIBIT AREA CLOSED** EXTINCT

In the top cage, draw or write the names of extinct animals.

ENDANGERED SPECIES

In the scene above, draw or write the names of animals that are in danger of extinction.

NEWSPAPER FOR PRETEENS THAT WANT TO TAKE CARE OF CREATION

Vol. 1 N°

CARE FOR IT!

WHY SHOULD WE TAKE CARE OF OUR WORLD?

WHAT CAN WE DO TO TAKE CARE OF OUR WORLD?

EVALUATION CARD

	GOOD	NORMAL	BAD
Plants			
Animals			
Fish			
Birds			
Water			
Atmosphere			
Natural Resources			
Comments			

Lesson 28

A DIFFERENT LIFE

From this...

Why was John called the "Son of Thunder"?

Mark 9:38-40
Mark 10:35-43
Luke 9:51-56

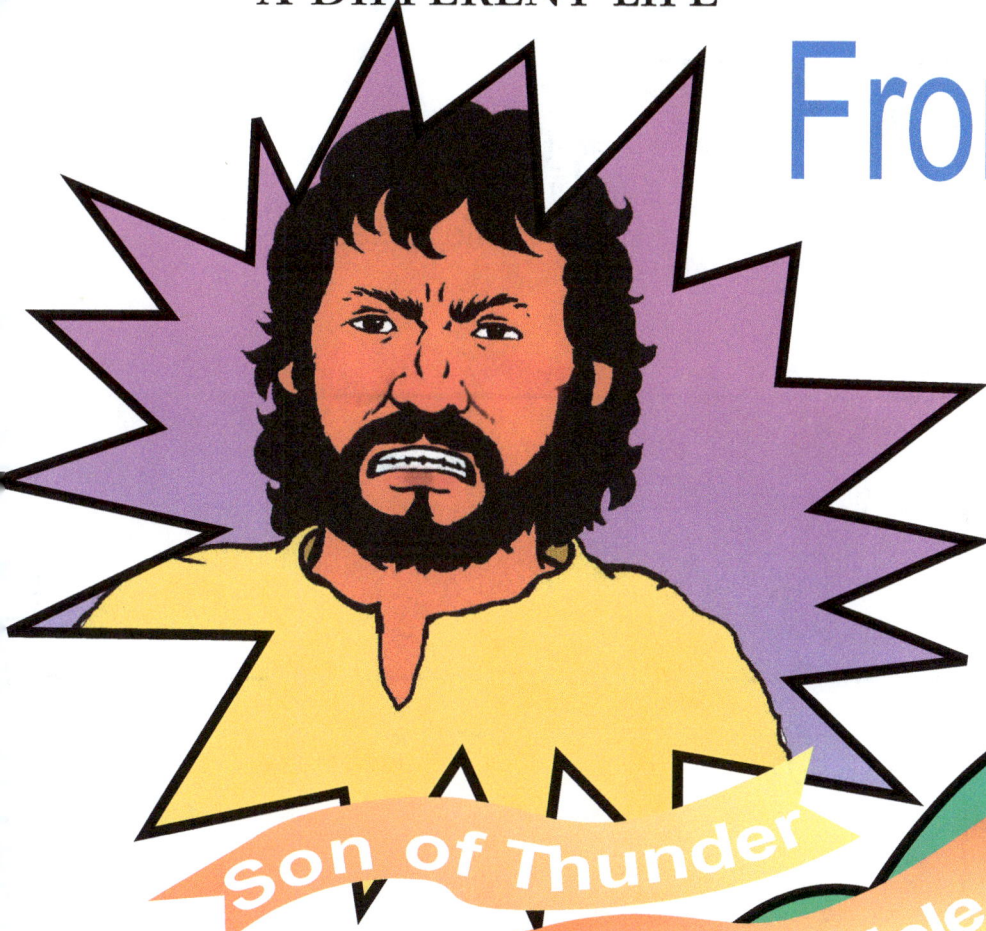

Son of Thunder

Beloved Disciple

How do we know that John was loved by Jesus?

John 19:25-27
John 20:1-9

TO THIS

103

EVIDENCE

... in the Life of John

Read the verses and explain how the change in John's life is seen.

1 John 2:16-17.

John wanted an important position in the Kingdom of God.

1 John 5:14.

John had a selfish attitude.

1 John 4:19-21.

John wanted revenge on the Samaritans who rejected Jesus.

1 John 1:9.

John's attitude was not always like Christ's.

OF CHANGE

...in the life of preteens

Describe a preteen who has a problem similar to John's.

Example of a problem caused when someone wants to be important:

Carlos wanted to be the best player on the team and to score the most goals. His team lost scoring opportunities because he did not want to pass the ball to his teammates. The other players got mad at Carlos for the way he played.

Example of a problem caused by selfishness:

Example of a problem caused by the desire to get revenge:

Example of a problem caused by non-Christian attitudes:

"But if we walk in the light, as he is in the light, we have fellowship with one another, and the blood of Jesus, his Son, purifies us from all sin." (1 John 1:7)

All About John!

This girl has prepared cards to tell us about the most important events of John's life and his writings. Read them carefully to know more about this disciple.

1. LIFE OF JOHN BEFORE JESUS

- Son of Zebedee.
- Brother of James.
- Fisherman.
- Lived near the Sea of Galilee.

2. LIFE OF JOHN WITH JESUS

- Jesus called him to be his disciple.
- He was with Jesus when He healed Jairus' daughter.
- He was in the garden of Gethsemane.
- He was at the crucifixion of Jesus.
- He saw Jesus ascend to heaven.

3. LIFE OF JOHN AFTER JESUS

- He took care of Jesus' mother.
- He wrote 5 of the New Testament books.
- He was imprisoned for the cause of Christ.

4. BOOKS BY JOHN

- The Gospel of John: proclaims that Jesus is the Son of God.
- 1 John: talks about the love of God; He asks us to love God and others.
- 2 John.
- 3 John.
- Revelation: talks about future events and of heave

5. JOHN'S UNIQUE STYLE OF WRITING

- He wrote about his personal experiences.
- He referred to God as "love".
- He referred to Jesus as "the Word."
- He spoke about the Holy Spirit and the second coming of Christ.

Where can you find John's books?

Color with a soft tone the five books that John wrote. Cut out this strip and use it as a bookmark in your Bible while you study the writings of John.

MATTHEW
MARK
LUKE
JOHN
ACTS
ROMANS
1 CORINTHIANS
2 CORINTHIANS
GALATIANS
EPHESIANS
COLOSSIANS
1 THESSALONIANS
2 THESSALONIANS
1 TIMOTHY
2 TIMOTHY
TITUS
PHILEMON
HEBREWS
JAMES
1 PETER
2 PETER
1 JOHN
2 JOHN
3 JOHN
JUDE
REVELATION

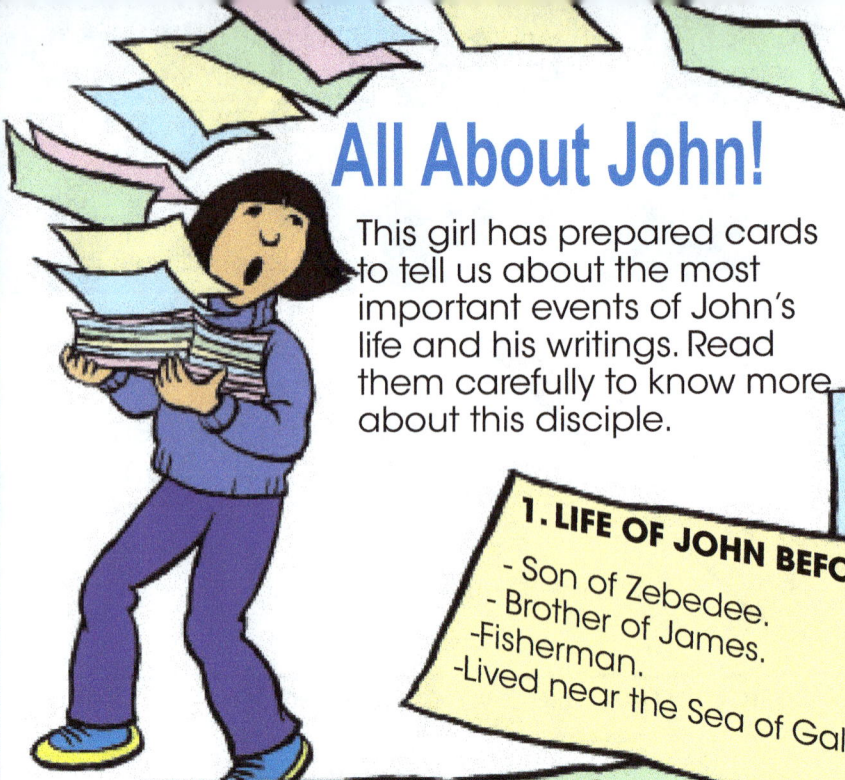

LET'S LIVE LIKE JESUS

WALK IN THE LIGHT

What does it mean?

Read the following verses and reflect: What does it mean to walk in light?

Walk with God after your sins are forgiven.
(1 John 1:7)

Live in obedience to the teachings of Jesus.
(1 John 2:6)

Love all people.
(1 John 2:10)

Love God above everything else.
(1 John 2:15-17)

WHAT DOES THE BIBLE SAY?

Read 1 John 1:5-10; 2:1-11.
Connect each verse with its meaning.

1. "This is the message we have heard from him and declare to you: God is light; in him there is no darkness at all."

   (1 John 1:5)

A person can not have fellowship with God while living in sin. If someone says they can, they are lying.

2. "If we claim to have fellowship with him and yet walk in the darkness, we lie and do not live out the truth."

   (1 John 1:6)

Light and darkness are spiritual terms to represent righteousness and sin. God is pure and holy. In him there is no sin.

3. "But if we walk in the light, as he is in the light, we have fellowship with one another, and the blood of Jesus, his Son, purifies us from all sin."

   (1 John 1:7)

Sin is contrary to the nature of God. Christians should not sin. But if a Christian does sin, Jesus Christ will speak to the Father for that person.

4. "My dear children, I write this to you so that you will not sin. But if anybody does sin, we have an advocate with the Father—Jesus Christ, the Righteous One."

   (1 John 2:1)

Everyone who claims to be a Christian, but hates another person, is living in sin.

5. "But if anyone obeys his word, love for God is truly made complete in them. This is how we know we are in him: Whoever claims to live in him must live as Jesus did."

   (1 John 2:5-6)

If a person decides to stop sinning, they are forgiven through Jesus' sacrifice. Then, that person can have a good relationship with God and with other Christians.

6. "Anyone who claims to be in the light but hates a brother or sister is still in the darkness."

   (1 John 2:9)

We can be sure of our relationship with God if we obey his commandments and live as Jesus taught us.

"But if we walk in the light, as he is in the light, we have fellowship with one another, and the blood of Jesus, his Son, purifies us from all sin." (1 John 1:7)

Those who says they abide in him must walk as he walked.

(1 John 2:6)

What was Jesus' attitude towards the people around him?

What is your attitude towards your heavenly Father?

How should I live to be more like Jesus?

Lesson 30

LOVE IS THE KEY

Different Kinds of Love

How do they compare to our love for God?

Love for Friends

Love for Grand-parents

LET'S LEARN
MORE ABOUT LOVE

**Use this concordance to answer
the following questions:**

1 John	2:5	**L** for God is truly made complete in them
	2:15	Do not **L** the world or anything in the world.
	3:1	what great **L** the Father has lavished on us
	3:10	nor is anyone who does not **L** their brother and sister.
	3:16	This is how we know what **L** is
	3:18	let us not **L** with words or speech
	4:9	this is how God showed his **L**
	4:10	This is **L**:
	4:11	we also ought to **L** love one another.
	4:16	God is **L**
	4:19	We **L** because he first loved us
	5:3	this is **L** for God: to keep his commands
2 John	6:1	this is **L**: that we walk in obedience to his commands

Decide which references go along with each question.
Then read the verses in the Bible and write your answers.

1. How is the love of God perfected?

2. How great is God's love?

3. How do we know what love is?

4. How do we show our love to God?

5. How can others know that we love God?

God Showed Us His Love

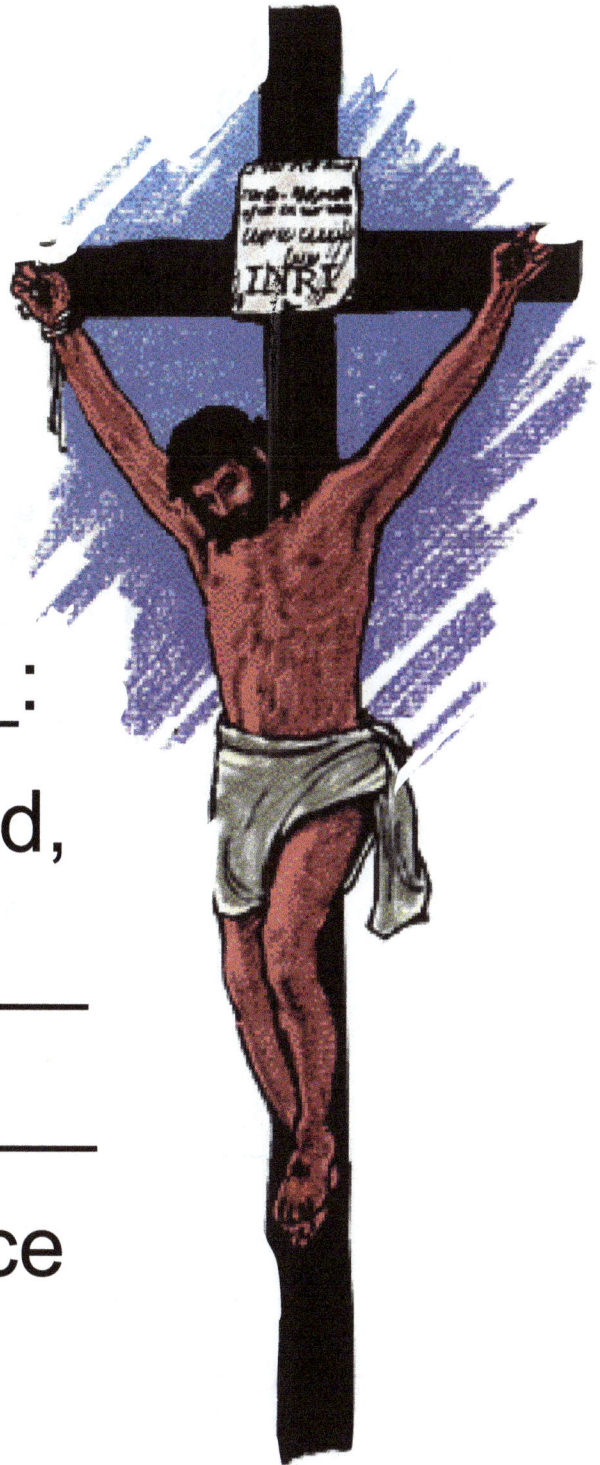

Complete the verse.

"This is _____:
not that we loved God,
but that he loved _____
and sent his _____
as an atoning sacrifice
for our _____."

(1 John 4:10)

How can preteens show their love to God?

Always Remember!

LOVE IS:

_____ when someone offends you.

_____ when you have offended someone.

_____ to those who are rejected by others.

_____ God's love to everyone you know.

Love is this and much, much more!

How would you define love?

> "Dear friends, since God so loved us, we also ought to love one another."
>
> *(1 John 4:11)*

114

WHAT DO WE BELIEVE?

I BELIEVE

or not?

Read the following religious beliefs of various groups. Put an X next to those that do not agree with the Word of God.

1 We believe in God. His name is Jehovah. Jesus, the Son of God, was the first being that Jehovah created. Before transferring his life to a human being, he was the archangel Michael. He taught that salvation is obtained by doing good works.

2 We believe in God, the Father of this world. Our church teaches how God came to be God. Before he was like us, flesh and blood. We can be like him and become gods. Jesus was human too. He was special because he was the firstborn of God. However, Jesus is not unique. We can all be like him!

Continue ▶

3 We believe in one God, the only true God. Our God is triune, that is, three persons but one God: God the Father, God the Son and God the Holy Spirit. God always was and always will be. Jesus Christ, God the Son, died for our sins. God raised him from the dead. Only by faith in Christ can our sins be forgiven.

4 We believe in God, the omniscient, who is full of love. Jesus was a man who introduced Christ (the true idea of God) to the world. Jesus was special because he represented the true idea of God better than anyone.

5 We believe in Jesus Christ. He came to earth to save men. However, Jesus didn't finish his work. After he died on the cross, his disciples turned him into God.

6 We believe in Christ. In all of us there is an awareness of God, a Christ. We must find Christ within us.

Which of these statements is consistent with what John wrote, which was inspired by God?

Which of these statements is consistent with the statement of the first Christians in the Apostles' Creed?

Lesson 32

WHO IS THE HOLY SPIRIT?

[Jesus said:] "And I will ask the Father, and he will give you another advocate to help you and be with you forever— the Spirit of truth. The world cannot accept him, because it neither sees him nor knows him. But you know him, for he lives with you and will be in you." (John 14:16-17)

The Holy Spirit

The Holy Spirit is one of the three Persons of the Trinity. God is revealed to us through the Holy Spirit. "Paraclete" is a Greek term that John used to refer to the Holy Spirit. It means: helper, comforter and advocate. The Holy Spirit is the one who teaches, encourages, helps and comforts us. The Holy Spirit helps sinners know about Christ and his gospel. The Holy Spirit guides sinners to receive salvation, helps them to have faith, and transforms those who believe in Christ. Christians are sinners who have repented of their sins and "are born of the Spirit." The Holy Spirit is the divine agent who sanctifies believers.

1. How is God revealed to people now?

2. What is the Greek word that refers to the Holy Spirit?

3. What are the three meanings of Paraclete?

4. Write four ways in which the Holy Spirit helps Christians.

How does the Holy Spirit help us?

1. What makes this sailboat move on water?

2. What would happen if the wind stopped blowing?

3. The Bible tells us that the Holy Spirit is like the wind. In fact, the Greek word that translates as "Spirit" is the same as the word used for "wind." How is the Holy Spirit similar to the wind in this illustration?

1. What makes these leaves move?

2. How do we know that the wind is blowing if we can't see it?

3. How is this similar to the work of the Holy Spirit in our lives?

1. Why does the young man in the second picture look more relaxed and calm?

2. How would that young man feel without the air conditioning?

3. What would our life be like if we did not have the comforting presence of the Holy Spirit?

1. Why are these rocks shaped the way they are?

2. How long do you think it took for the wind to produce these rock formations?

3. If we compare the Holy Spirit with the wind, what does this illustration teach us about the work of the Holy Spirit in our life?

HELP FOR PRETEENS

Lately, some friends of Deborah's have gotten involved in activities that bother her. Her best friend Marcia smokes on the way from school to the house. One day at the mall, Deborah's friends offered her a cigarette. Deborah is afraid that if she doesn't accept the cigarette, they will think she is very proud. Also, since she went with them to the mall, she doesn't want them to get angry and leave her there.

How is the Holy Spirit helping Deborah?

How will the Holy Spirit help her if she gives in to temptation and smokes?

How will the Holy Spirit help her if she stands firm and defends what is right?

Mark is a popular young man at school and a sanctified Christian. Recently a new student arrived who dresses and speaks differently than the other students. Most of Mark's classmates make fun of the new kid. Mark feels uncomfortable when he sees how the new student is being treated.

How is the Holy Spirit helping Mark?

How will the Holy Spirit help him if he gives in to temptation and makes fun of the new kid?

How will the Holy Spirit help Mark if he decides to offer his friendship to the new kid?

What would the Holy Spirit do?

		RESPONSE 1	RESPONSE 2	RESPONSE 3
SITUATION 1	Your mom asks you to clean off the table. You are doing something else, so you answer, "I'm coming." After asking you many times and you still don't do it, she forbids you from going out with your friends for a week. **What will the Holy Spirit do?**	Will the Holy Spirit make you feel like you're worthless for disobeying your parents?	Will the Holy Spirit support you and say that nobody can tell you what to do?	Will the Holy Spirit remind you to obey your parents and encourage you to ask for forgiveness?

		RESPONSE 1	RESPONSE 2	RESPONSE 3
SITUATION 2	You wake up in a bad mood because you went to bed late last night. Now you must get up and go to school. Since you feel so grumpy, you wonder if you are still a Christian. **What will the Holy Spirit do?**	Will the Holy Spirit condemn you for feeling grumpy, or encourage you to be happy because you're a Christian?	Will the Holy Spirit tell you that a Christian doesn't experience those feelings?	Will the Holy Spirit tell you that if you are forgiven and are following God, you don't have to worry about "feeling" like a Christian all the time?

		RESPONSE 1	RESPONSE 2	RESPONSE 3
SITUATION 3	Your Sunday School teacher encouraged you to read the Bible every day. You've tried to many times, but you don't always understand it, so it's hard for you to have your daily devotions. **What will the Holy Spirit do?**	Will the Holy Spirit remind you that you are not smart enough to understand the Bible?	Will the Holy Spirit suggest that you wait to read the Bible until you grow up and can better understand it?	Will the Holy Spirit help you understand what you read in the Bible?

THE HOLY SPIRIT TEACHES US

What do they teach me?

Write the
name of:

Five popular

SONGS

Five popular

MAGAZINES

Five popular

GAMES

WHAT DO YOU LEARN FROM THEM?

121

WHAT DOES THE BIBLE SAY?

Choose someone from your group to read the Bible passage. Then, answer the questions?

Read John 14:15-19, 26.

1. Who speaks in this passage?

2. Why is verse 15 important?

3. Why can't the world accept the Holy Spirit?

4. What will the Holy Spirit teach us?

Read John 16:7-15.

1. Who speaks in this passage?

2. What will the Holy Spirit do?

3. What will the Holy Spirit teach us?

Read 2 Corinthians 1:21-22.

1. Who gives us the Holy Spirit?

2. According to verse 21, what does God do?

3. What has God given us as a guarantee in our hearts?

122

What could the Holy Spirit teach us in these situations? Should you do something different the next time?

What Happened?

For me it is difficult to talk about Jesus to my friends; most of them do not go to church. I felt I should invite them, so on Sunday I prayed, asking the Holy Spirit to show me the right time and place to ask them. This morning I felt it was time, so I invited my friend Kurt. You know what? He said he would like to go with me! Now I feel ashamed for having felt so afraid.

I know I should not spend time with people who invite me to do bad things. But I read in the Bible that the Holy Spirit will protect me from bad influences. He will not let me be tempted more than I can bear. So, what's the problem if I hang out with those people? I can face them!

The Holy Spirit helps me make good decisions. So the other day when I faced a temptation, I asked God not to let me fall. Since the Holy Spirit didn't stop me, I assumed there was no problem doing it. So, why did my parents get so angry?

Holy Spirit
teach me

Make a list of the things you want the Holy Spirit to teach you.

1.

2.

3.

4.

5.

[Jesus said:] "But the Advocate, the Holy Spirit, whom the Father will send in my name, will teach you all things and will remind you of everything I have said to you." (John 14:26)

THE HOLY SPIRIT GUIDES US

Can you follow these instructions?

The following statements suggest simple and common activities. Read the instructions and decipher what the activity is.

1. Through the process of exhalation, making a combination of oxygen, nitrogen, and carbon dioxide pass through the oral cavity, contracting both labia oris, which have an outer mucosa with a stratified epithelial surface.

2. Using your orbicularis oculi muscle, make your oculus dexter be posterior to your palpebra.

3. Flexing the portion of your trunk between the ribs and the pelvis, point to your left hallux with the digitus minimus of your dominant manus.

4. Flex your two articulatio genus repeatedly while keeping both upper extremities extended laterally.

EASY

WHAT?

SIMPLE

THE JERUSALEM GAZETTE

IF IT'S IMPORTANT, YOU'LL READ ABOUT IT HERE!

THE CHRISTIAN COUNCIL MEETS

Division in the Church is Avoided

The Jerusalem Council established a standard for resolving disputes peacefully and prayerfully. These disagreement could have divided the church and ruined its future.

The people attending the meeting were happy with the results. Jewish Christians agreed that faith in Jesus Christ is the only requirement to be children of God. Gentile Christians agreed to accept the following Jewish requirements:

1. Refrain from food sacrificed to idols.
2. Maintain sexual purity
3. Refrain from eating meat from a strangled animal and blood.

Jewish standards are much higher than those of pagan society.

The Council sent two representatives, Judas (called Barsabbas) and Silas, with a letter explaining the decision to the Christians of Antioch. These men traveled with Paul and Barnabas.

In the church of Antioch, the message was read for all to hear, and it caused the people to rejoice. Then, Barsabbas and Silas returned to their tasks in the city of Jerusalem.

JERUSALEM "The Friendly City"

The Chamber of Commerce of Jerusalem wishes to promote our city as "Jerusalem, The Friendly City". Thousands of visitors come to this city every year to trade. Our leaders want them to feel welcome and want to return.

This week, visitors from Antioch arrived to hold a church meeting. The president of the Chamber of Commerce hopes that you will enjoy your visit, and when you return to Antioch, tell your friends that Jerusalem is a wonderful place to visit.

127

HOLY SPIRIT GUIDE ME!

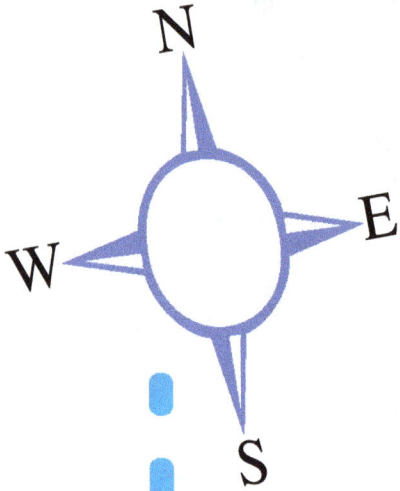

1. Mention specific areas in which you would like the Holy Spirit to guide you this week.

2. Choose one of the areas you mentioned in the previous point and explain what you want the Holy Spirit to do.

3. What advice would you recognize, without a doubt, as something that does not come from the Holy Spirit?

4. How do you think the Holy Spirit will guide you to do?

5. What is your responsibility when the guidance of the Holy Spirit is clear?

"But when he, the Spirit of truth, comes, he will guide you into all the truth." (*John 16:13a*)

THE HOLY SPIRIT GIVES US POWER

COULD YOU

DO THIS ?

Read this story and answer the questions.

Operation Auca was a very dangerous missionary adventure for Jim Elliot and four other missionaries. They went to Ecuador, a country in South America, to the region where the tribe of the Auca Indians lived. Jim was sure that God had led him to tell the Aucas about Jesus.

After several months of throwing gifts from a plane, Jim, his friend Nate Saint and three other missionaries established a missionary camp in the area where the Aucas lived. Soon they began to communicate with them. They were excited about the possibilities of evangelizing the Auca people.

However, suddenly something happened that is difficult to understand. On January 8, 1956, the Aucas killed the five missionaries.

- If you were a relative of one of the missionaries, what would you have felt towards the Aucas?

- Do you think the missionaries were following God's guidance? Why or why not?

The story could have ended here. This event could have been considered as a total tragedy, without any positive value.

However, a few years later, certain people returned to the same area to share the Gospel with the Aucas (they even translated the Gospel of Mark into the language of the Aucas). Can you guess who returned? It was Elizabeth Elliot, the widow of Jim Elliot. She came back to preach the gospel to the people who had killed her husband.

- Who gave Elizabeth Elliot power to do what she did?

- What would you have done in that situation?

Read Acts 6:8 - 7:1, 51-60, and respond to the questions assigned to your group.

Why didn't he defend himself?

1. Did someone ever tell a lie about you? How did that change your relationship with that person?

2. How do you react when someone mistreats you?

3. Based on the passage, how would you describe Stephen?

4. In what ways are you like Stephen?

5. Why did Stephen call the Sanhedrin "stiff-neck people"? What does it mean?

6. What does it mean to "resist the Holy Spirit"?

7. Why did Stephen's words make members of the council so angry?

8. According to verse 60, what characteristics do you see in Stephen?

9. Why could Stephen respond like he did?

10. Why didn't Stephen defend himself?

11. What can you do this week to be more like Stephen?

"But you will receive power when the Holy Spirit comes on you; and you will be my witnesses in Jerusalem, and in all Judea and Samaria, and to the ends of the earth."

(Acts 1:8)

ISRAEL HAS A KING

What makes a Friendship Last?

What does God require in our relationship with him?

Start

Read Deuteronomy 10:12 (NIV). Then find the path through the labyrinth, by following the words of the verse in order.

so	obedience	to	faith	to	down	so	John	Lord
do	in	me	him,	love	to	joy	the	your
And	joy	walk	die	him,	he	serve	sin	God
just	now,	John	to	Jesus	do	one	with	only
he	only	Israel,	holy	God,	so	all	die	love
did	you	sin	what	your	your	faith	and	me
but	Jesus	of	Lord	does	he	heart	with	your
to	holy	the	ask	obey	the	joy	all	soul..."
sin	fear	spirit	do	God	John	Lord	just	Dt.
love	Bible	faith	only	me	your	one	Jesus	10:12

Name **four** requirements to have a good relationship with God.

What was Israel's Attitude?

1. Why did the Israelites want to have a king?

2. What does 1 Samuel 8:7-9 tell us about Israel's obedience to God?

3. How did the Israelites respond to the warnings? (1 Samuel 8:19-20)

4. Did the Israelites fulfill God's commands?

Did Saul fulfill God's commands?

What was Saul's Attitude?

1 Samuel	
9:3-4	*he cared for others*
9:5	*humble*
9:21; 10:22	*brave*
10:6, 9	*obeyed authority*
10:27	*he was not vindictive*
11:6, 11	*gave credit to God*
11:13	*was transformed by God*

Do you want to start a relationship with God?

1 ADMIT that you have sinned.

2 REPENT of your sin.

3 DECIDE that you will stop sinning.

4 ASK God to forgive you.

You can pray right now!

Dear God:
I admit that I have sinned, and I regret all the bad things I've done. I ask you to forgive me. I believe that Jesus died for me on the cross and I accept Him as my Lord and Savior. Help me to obey you always. Thank you for forgiving me and making me your child. In the name of Jesus. Amen.

What can I do to strengthen my relationship with God?

THE KING DISOBEYS GOD

HE MUST

Characters: Narrator, Saul, Samuel, Jonathan, captain of the army

Scene 1: On the battlefield.

Saul: Jonathan, we have 3,000 strong and brave warriors. I don't think we'll have any problems the next time we fight the Philistines.

Jonathan: Our informants say that there is a group of Philistines on the hill. Father, why don't we go with 1,000 soldiers and attack them? The others can stay behind in case of a surprise attack.

Saul: I think that's a good idea, Jonathan. Go and may God be with you.

Narrator: Jonathan attacked the enemy army in Gibeah. When the Philistines heard about it, they gathered their armies to fight against Israel. Saul sent word to the Israelites that they should meet at Gilgal for battle.

Scene 2: In Gilgal.

Saul: You did a good job, son, but now the Philistines are very angry. Let's go to the top of that hill. From there we can see how many have gathered in the valley.

Army Captain: King Saul, look! There must be at least 3,000 chariots and 6,000 charioteers and soldiers as numerous as the sand on the seashore. What will we do? We can not defend ourselves with only 3,000 men.

Jonathan: Our soldiers are very scared! Some have hidden in caves and pits. And others fled!

Army Captain: Where is Samuel? He said he would come. He is supposed to offer a sacrifice to ensure that God is with us.

Saul: We can't wait! The Philistines will attack us at any moment and they will surely kill us all. I will offer the sacrifice.

Jonathan: What are you saying? Only priests can offer sacrifices.

Saul: We can not wait any longer.

Narrator: Saul began offering the sacrifice. Just as he had finished making the sacrifice, Samuel arrived.

Samuel: (sniffing the air) Smells like burned flesh.

Saul: Samuel, where were you? We waited for you for a long time. The Philistines are ready to attack us and my soldiers were scattering in fear. That's why I went ahead and offered the sacrifice without you to ask for God's help.

WAIT!

135

Samuel: Saul, what foolishness! If you had obeyed God, one of your descendants would have been king after you. Now even you will not stay on the throne for long.

Narrator: Some time later, God commanded Saul to fight against the Amalekites. He told him to destroy all their possessions so that nothing contaminated the Israelites.

Scene 3: After the battle with the Amalekites

Army Captain: King Saul, we won the battle. Hey, the king of the Amalekites is fleeing! What should do we do with him?

Saul: God told me to destroy all the enemy's possessions. What a waste! I think the best thing is to take the king as a prisoner. Why don't we also take the best of the cattle? I do not think we should kill their animals; let's keep them for ourselves and we will become richer.

Narrator: The next morning Samuel went to Saul's camp to find out what had happened in the battle.

Saul: (showing off to Samuel) We won, Samuel! I did everything that God commanded me.

Samuel: Why do I hear so much noise? It seems like the bleat of sheep and the bellowing of cows.

Saul: Well, we brought the best of the Amalek sheep and cows ... but only to offer them as a sacrifices to God!

Narrator: Samuel knew that Saul was lying. God had already anticipated it.

Samuel: Do not say anything else! Last night God told me that you had disobeyed him. Now I see with my eyes what you have done. Don't you know that God prefers your obedience over your sacrifices? This is a warning: because you did not listen to God, you will not be king for long.

How do people try to compensate for the bad things they do?

Paula needed a good grade on her science test. Her parents had warned her that if her grade dropped any more, she would lose certain privileges at home.

The next day, Paula cheated on the exam by copying a friend's answers. Then she felt bad. When she went to church, she took the money she had been saving and put it in the offering plate. She thought maybe that would help her feel better.

Rick needed a book for his math homework. Since he was the last one to leave the classroom, he saw the book he needed on the teacher's desk and, without asking, took it home. After using it, he forgot the book on his bed; the dog found it and destroyed the cover.

The next day, Rick arrived earlier than everyone and put the book in its place. When the teacher saw that it was damaged, he got angry and asked who had done it. Nobody confessed.

Rick continued thinking about the book. He had disappointed God, his teacher and himself, so he decided to volunteer to cut the grass at the church on Saturday, instead of going to play with his friend Roger. He thought maybe volunteering at church would make him feel better.

137

"Then Saul said to Samuel, 'I have sinned. I violated the Lord's command and your instructions. I was afraid of the men and so I gave in to them.'"
(1 Samuel 15:24)
"If we confess our sins, he is faithful and just and will forgive us our sins and purify us from all unrighteousness."
(1 John 1:9)

FROM BAD TO WORSE

What's Going On ?

1 On Sunday Nate told his mother that he would clean his room, but because he was in a hurry to get to church, he decided not to do it.

2 On Monday, Nate forgot to do his math homework, so he decided to lie to the teacher telling him that he was sick over the weekend.

3 On Tuesday Nate told his dad that the teacher had not given homework, although it was not true. Actually, he had gotten distracted and forgot to copy it from the board.

4 On Wednesday, Nate' mother sent him to the store to buy something she needed. He took the opportunity and also bought some candies with his mother's money without her permission.

5 On Thursday Nate offered to help his friend Chris do math homework, but then he forgot and stayed after school to play ball with his friends.

6 On Friday, Nate's mother gave him the umbrella so he wouldn't get wet in the rain. He thought a little rain wouldn't hurt him and hid the umbrella when his mom wasn't around.

7 On Saturday, Nate promised his mother that he would help her clean the house, but then he decided he didn't want to, so he went and spent the day with his friend Kevin.

SAUL'S TERRIBLE Dilemma

Officer 1: What happened to the king?

Officer 2: I don't know, and I don't want to ask him. He is more and more quiet and he no longer trusts anyone.

Officer 1: You're right! It all started after David killed Goliath. Do you remember when the women came out to meet Saul? They sang: "Saul has slain his thousands, and David his tens of thousand." Until then everything was fine, but his jealousy began when he heard that song.

Officer 2: That's right! Saul could not stand it. He is afraid that David will take away his throne.

Officer 1: What was that?

Officer 2: I didn't hear anything. Keep telling me the story.

Officer 1: Do you remember how Saul tried to nail David to the wall with his spear?

Officer 2: Yes! David was playing his harp when suddenly, Saul threw his spear at him and almost killed him.

Official 1: However, David managed to escape from Saul twice.

Officer 2: It seemed that Saul wanted to make things right when he put David in charge of a thousand soldiers.

Officer 1: Yes, but you know that Saul only wanted David to die in the war. That's why he sent him, along with his men, to the battlefront.

Officer 2: But that only made the situation worse. David's exploits made him even more popular.

Officer 1: Can you believe that King Saul told David that he had to kill 100 Philistines to marry Princess Michel?

Officer 2: Saul was sure that would be the end of David.

Officer 1: But that didn't work either.

Officer 2: Saul is getting worse. He has become more difficult. Now he suspects everyone!

Officer 1: I couldn't believe it when he asked us to kill all the priests of God.

Officer 2: How could we do that!

Officer 1: But now everyone is hiding, just like David and his men. Who do you think could advise the king now that the Philistines are attacking us again?

Officer 2: I wish I knew.

WHAT WOULD HAVE HAPPENED?

GROUP 1

What would have happened if Saul had waited for Samuel to offer the sacrifice in Gilgal?

What would have happened if Saul had obeyed God's command to destroy the Amalekites?

What would have happened if Saul had accepted God's will for David to be the new king?

What would have happened if Saul had not visited the fortune-teller of Endor?

WHAT DID HAPPENED?

GROUP 2

What happened when Saul offered the sacrifice in Gilgal instead of waiting for Samuel?

What happened when Saul saved the best animals and took the Amalekite king as a prisoner?

What happened when Saul was jealous of David?

What happened when Saul asked the fortune teller of Endor for help?

What pattern of behavior do you follow?

What pattern of behavior is this person following?

Look back at the beginning of Lesson 38 and answer this question: What pattern of behavior is Nate following in his life? What could he do to correct it?

How do you behave each day? Do you have a good behavior pattern? If not, what can you do to change it?

142

"And now, Israel, what does the Lord your God ask of you but to fear the Lord your God, to walk in obedience to him, to love him, to serve the Lord your God with all your heart and with all your soul..."
(Deuteronomy 10:12)

CAN THERE BE A GOOD KING?

How do you RATE them?

1. Write an S above the arrow where you would rate Saul for each characteristic.
2. Write a D above the arrow where you would rate David for each characteristic.

The first one is done as an example.

IMPATIENT	S D ←——————→	PATIENT
LOVES HIMSELF	←——————————→	LOVES GOD
BLAMES OTHERS	←——————————→	RESPONSIBLE FOR HIS DECISIONS
DISOBEDIENT	←——————————→	OBEDIENT
FOLLOWS THE WORSHIP RITUALS	←——→	SERVES GOD WITH SINCERITY
DOESN'T HONOR GOD	←——→	RESPECTS GOD'S AUTHORITY
FEARED AND HATED	←——→	LOVED AND RESPECTED
CONTROLS HIS LIFE	←——→	ALLOWS GOD TO DIRECT HIS LIFE

143

Caught You!

Nobody likes to be caught doing something wrong. Read the following verses to see if they are talking about Saul or David. How were the reactions of Saul and David different when they sinned?

1 SAMUEL 15:13-16

1 SAMUEL 15:30

2 SAMUEL 11:14-15

1 SAMUEL 15:24-25

2 SAMUEL 12:5-7, 13

PSALM 51:1-4

OH, NO!

Have mercy on me, O God, according to your unfailing Love; according to your great compassion blot out my transgressions. Wash away all my iniquity and cleanse me from my sin. For I know my transgressions, and my sin is always before me. Against you, you only, have I sinned and done what is evil in your sight; so you are right in your verdict and justified when you judge.

Create in me a pure heart, O God, and renew a steadfast spirit within me. Do not cast me from your presence or take your Holy Spirit from me. Restore to me the joy of your salvation and grant me a willing spirit, to sustain me.

Open my lips, Lord, and my mouth will declare your praise. You do not delight in sacrifice, or I would bring it; you do not take pleasure in burnt offerings. My sacrifice, O God, is a broken spirit; a broken and contrite heart you, God, will not despise.

(Psalm 51:1-4, 10-12, 15-17)

145

Read the phrase that is in the center of the circle and the surrounding questions. Write your answers in the outer circle.

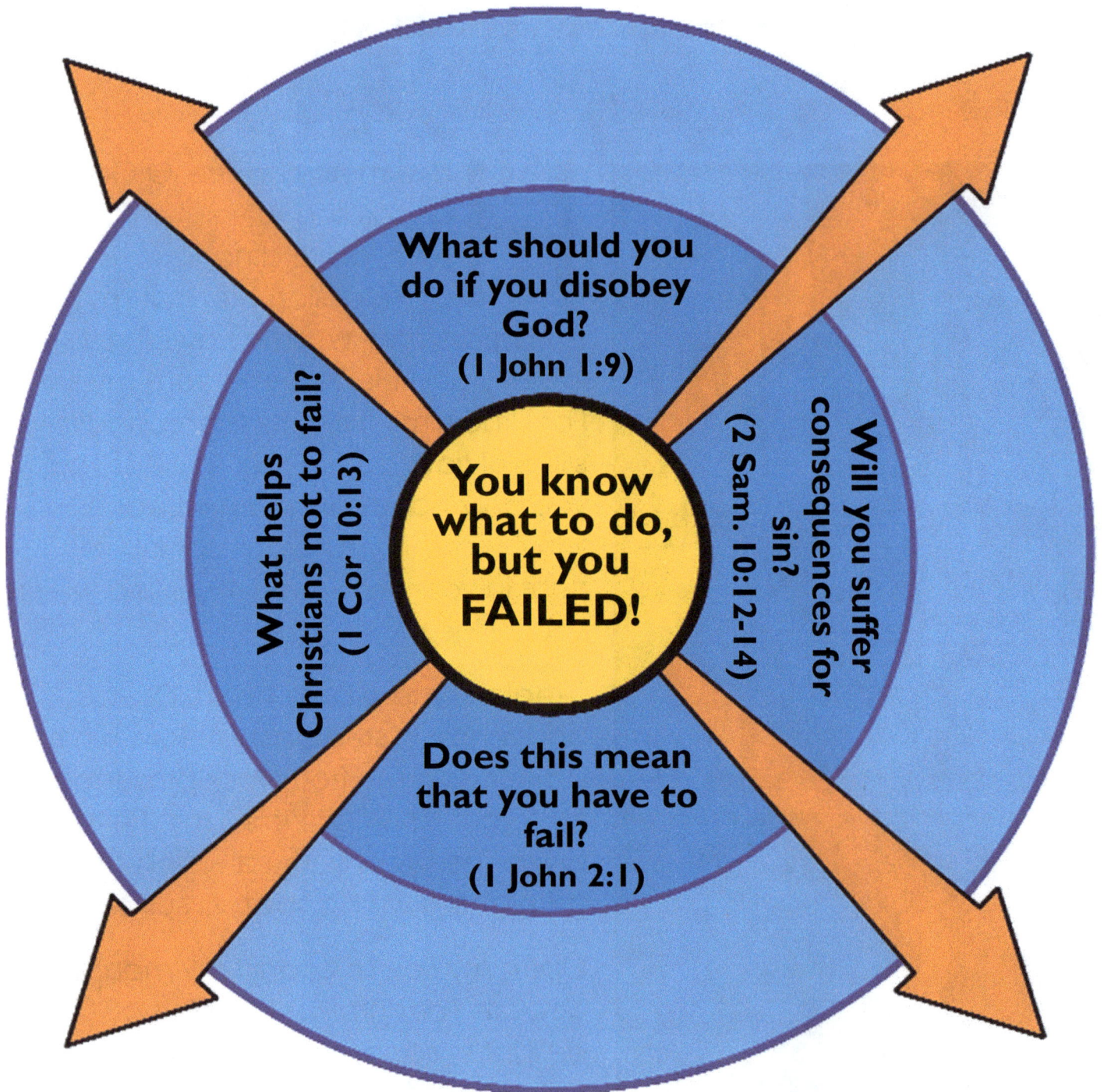

What should you do if you disobey God?
(1 John 1:9)

What helps Christians not to fail?
(1 Cor 10:13)

You know what to do, but you FAILED!

Will you suffer consequences for sin?
(2 Sam. 10:12-14)

Does this mean that you have to fail?
(1 John 2:1)

What Does God Ask of Christians?

THE FALL OF A WISE KING

WISDOM OF THE WORLD VS. WISDOM OF GOD

Have you ever heard your friends make any of the following statements? What kind of wisdom do they represent?

If you like it, then it must be ok.

If everyone does it, I can do it too.

Laws were made to be broken.

It's my life, and I will live it as I please.

Nobody can tell you what is good; Only you can decide.

God observes what happens in our lives from a different perspective.

PROMISES AND WARNINGS

God appeared to Solomon and he made a promise and gave a warning. Circle the promise. Underline the conditions for the promise. Underline the warning with a double line.

"As for you, if you walk before me faithfully with integrity of heart and uprightness, as David your father did, and do all I command, and observe my decrees and laws, I will establish your royal throne over Israel forever, as I promised David your father when I said, 'You shall never fail to have a successor on the throne of Israel.'

But if you or your descendants turn away from me and do not observe the commands and decrees I have given you and go off to serve other gods and worship them, then I will cut off Israel from the land I have given them and will reject this temple I have consecrated for my Name. Israel will then become a byword and an object of ridicule among all peoples."

(1 Kings 9:4-7)

Can there be a foolish wise person? Maybe you don't think that a wise person can do something foolish.

God gave Solomon more wisdom than any other person in the world.

Did all of his decisions reflect that wisdom? Read the following verses.

"So Solomon did evil in the eyes of the Lord; he did not follow the Lord completely, as David his father had done.

On a hill east of Jerusalem, Solomon built a high place for Chemosh the detestable god of Moab, and for Molek the detestable god of the Ammonites. He did the same for all his foreign wives, who burned incense and offered sacrifices to their gods.

The Lord became angry with Solomon because his heart had turned away from the Lord, the God of Israel, who had appeared to him twice. Although he had forbidden Solomon to follow other gods, Solomon did not keep the Lord's command."

(1 Kings 11:6-10)

A

WISE FOOL ?

CONSEQUENCES

COMPLETE THESE VERSES.

"So the Lord said to Solomon, 'Since this is your _____ and you have not _____ my covenant and my decrees, which I commanded you, I will most certainly _____ the kingdom away from you and _____ it to one of your subordinates. Nevertheless, for the sake of _____ your father, I will not do it during your _____. I will tear it out of the hand of your _____. Yet I will not tear the _____ kingdom from him, but will give him one _____ for the sake of David my _____ and for the sake of _____, which I have chosen.'"

149

(1 Kings 11:11-13)

ISRAEL

The Assyrian Empire Thrives

DIVIDED KINGDOM

Lessons from Three Kings

Review the stories of this unit and answer the following questions.

1. Name each character or event, and tell why they are important in the Bible story.

2. Describe the relationship that each character had with God.

3. Discuss what you learned from each character that will help you in your relationship with God.

4. What did each story teach you about God?

WHAT IS HAPPINESS?

JESUS SAID:

"_____ are the poor in _____, for theirs is the kingdom of heaven."
(Matthew 5:3)

"Blessed are the _____, for they will inherit the earth."
(Matthew 5:5)

DAVID SAID:

"But the _____ will inherit the land and enjoy peace and _____."
(Psalm 37:11)

PETER SAID:

"_____ yourselves, therefore, under God's mighty hand, that he may lift you up in due time. Cast all your _____ on him because he cares for you."
(1 Peter 5:6-7)

NOW I TELL YOU

_____

_____

_____

_____

_____

LUCAS 13. 20

La parábola de la levadura
Mt 13. 33

20 Dijo también: «¿Con qué podré comparar el Reino de Dios? 21 Se parece a un poco de levadura que una mujer mezcló con gran cantidad de harina, hasta que fermentó toda la masa».

Los nuevos elegidos del Reino
Mt 7. 13-14. 22-23; 25. 10-12
Mt 8. 11-12; 19. 30, 20. 16

22 Jesús iba enseñando por las ciudades y pueblos, mientras se dirigía a Jerusalén. 23 Una persona le preguntó: «Señor, ¿es verdad que son pocos los que se salvan?». El respondió: 24 «Traten de entrar por la puerta estrecha, porque les aseguro que muchos querrán entrar y no lo conseguirán. 25 En cuanto el dueño de casa se levante y cierre la puerta, ustedes, desde afuera, se pondrán a golpear la puerta, diciendo: "Señor, ábrenos". Y él les responderá: "No sé de dónde son ustedes". 26 Entonces comenzarán a decir: "Hemos comido y bebido contigo, y tú enseñaste en nuestras plazas". 27 Pero él les dirá: "No sé de dónde son ustedes; ¡apártense de mí todos los que hacen el mal!".

28 Allí habrá llantos y rechinar de dientes, cuando vean a Abraham, a Isaac, a Jacob y a todos los profetas en el Reino de Dios, y ustedes sean arrojados afuera. 29 Y vendrán muchos de Oriente y de Occidente, del Norte y del Sur, a ocupar su lugar en el banquete del Reino de Dios. 30 Hay algunos que son los últimos y serán los primeros, y hay otros que son los primeros y serán los últimos».

Actitud de Jesús ante la amenaza de Herodes

31 En ese momento se acercaron algunos fariseos que le dijeron: «Aléjate de aquí, porque Herodes quiere matarte». 32 El les

27. Sal. 6. 9.
28. Rechinar de dientes: ver nota Mt. 8. 12
31-33. Herodes temía que la actividad de Jesús provocara una agitación en sus dominios, y por eso trata de alejarlo con una amenaza. Los fariseos dan a Jesús un consejo aparentemente benévolo, aunque tal vez no haya que excluir una cierta complicidad con el tetrarca. Pero Jesús responde diciendo que la estratagema es inútil: la astucia humana —expresada en el epi-

respondió: «Vayan a decir a ese zorro: hoy y mañana expulso a los demonios y realizo curaciones, y al tercer día habré terminado. 33 Pero debo seguir mi camino hoy, mañana y pasado, porque no puede ser que un profeta muera fuera de Jerusalén».

Reproche de Jesús a Jerusalén
Mt 23. 37-39

34 ¡Jerusalén, Jerusalén, que matas a los profetas y apedreas a los que te son enviados! ¡Cuántas veces quise reunir a tus hijos, como la gallina reúne bajo sus alas a los pollitos, y tú no quisiste! 35 Por eso, a ustedes la casa les quedará vacía. Les aseguro que ya no me verán más, hasta que llegue el día en que digan:

¡Bendito el que viene
en nombre del Señor!».

Curación de un hidrópico en sábado
Mt 12. 11

14 1 Un sábado, Jesús entró a comer en casa de uno de los principales fariseos. Ellos lo observaban atentamente. 2 Delante de él había un hombre enfermo de hidropesía. 3 Jesús preguntó a los doctores de la Ley y a los fariseos: «¿Está permitido curar en sábado o no?». 4 Pero ellos guardaron silencio. Entonces Jesús tomó de la mano al enfermo, lo curó y lo despidió. 5 Y volviéndose hacia ellos, les dijo: «Si a alguno de ustedes se le cae en un pozo su hijo o su buey, ¿acaso no lo saca en seguida, aunque sea sábado?». 6 A esto no pudieron responder nada.

La humildad cristiana
Mt 23. 12

7 Y al notar cómo los invitados buscaban los primeros puestos, les dijo esta parábola: 8 «Si te invitan a un banquete de bodas, no te coloques en el primer lugar, porque

teto «zorro» aplicado a Herodes— no puede impedir el cumplir la misión que el Padre le ha confiado. «Hoy y mañana», es decir, durante un breve tiempo, el deber continuar curando enfermos y expulsando demonios. Después, «al tercer día», irá a Jerusalén para morir y dar así pleno cumplimiento a su misión. Ver nota Jn. 9. 4.
35. Sal. 118. 26 Ver 1 Rey. 9. 7-8. Jer 12 7. 22. 5

puede suceder que haya sido invitada otra persona más importante que tú. 9 Y cuando llegue el que los invitó a los dos, tenga que decirte: "Déjale el sitio", y así, lleno de vergüenza, tengas que ponerte en el último lugar. 10 Al contrario, cuando te inviten, ve a colocarte en el último puesto, de manera que cuando llegue el que te invitó, te diga: "Amigo, acércate más", y así, quedarás delante de todos los invitados. 11 Porque todo el que se ensalza será humillado, y el que se humilla será ensalzado».

12 Después dijo al que lo había invitado: «Cuando des un almuerzo o una cena, no invites a tus amigos, ni a tus hermanos, ni a tus parientes, ni a los vecinos ricos, no sea que ellos te inviten a su vez, y ésta sea tu recompensa. 13 Al contrario, cuando des un banquete, invita a los pobres, a los lisiados, a los paralíticos, a los ciegos. 14 ¡Feliz de ti, porque ellos no tienen cómo retribuirte, y así tendrás tu recompensa en la resurrección de los justos!».

La parábola de los invitados descorteses
Mt 22. 1-10

15 Al oír estas palabras, uno de los invitados le dijo: «¡Feliz el que se siente a la mesa en el Reino de Dios!». 16 Jesús respondió: «Un hombre preparó un gran banquete y convidó a mucha gente. 17 A la hora de cenar, mandó a su servidor a decir a los invitados: "Vengan, todo está preparado". 18 Pero todos, sin excepción, empezaron a excusarse. El primero le dijo: "Acabo de comprar un campo y tengo que ir a verlo. Te ruego me disculpes". 19 El segundo dijo: "He comprado cinco yuntas de bueyes y voy a probarlos. Te ruego me disculpes". 20 Y un tercero respondió: "Acabo de casarme y por esa razón no puedo ir". 21 A su regreso, el servidor contó todo esto al dueño de casa, y éste, irritado, le dijo: "Recorre en seguida las plazas y las calles de la ciudad, y trae aquí a los pobres, a los lisiados, a los ciegos y a los paralíticos". 22 Volvió el servidor y dijo: "Señor, tus órdenes se han cumplido y aún

23 El señor le respondió: "Ve a los caminos y a lo largo de los cercos, e insiste a la gente para que entre, de manera que se llene mi casa. 24 Porque les aseguro que ninguno de los que antes fueron invitados ha de probar mi cena"».

26. Ver...
33. Este...
tar las dos co...

> When he [Jesus] noticed how the guests picked the places of honor at the table, he told them this parable: "When someone invites you to a wedding feast, do not take the place of honor, for a person more distinguished than you may have been invited. If so, the host who invited both of you will come and say to you, 'Give this person your seat.' Then, humiliated, you will have to take the least important place. But when you are invited, take the lowest place, so that when your host comes, he will say to you, 'Friend, move up to a better place.' Then you will be honored in the presence of all the other guests. For all those who exalt themselves will be humbled, and those who humble themselves will be exalted."
>
> *(Luke 14:7-11)*

LOOK CLOSER!

ANSWER THESE QUESTIONS:

1. What motivated Jesus to tell this parable?

2. What happened to the person who sat in the place of honor?

3. What could happen to the person who sat in the place of less importance?

4. How could this parable be taken to an extreme?

5. What lesson do you learn from this parable?

CREATE A STORY!

What do you think is happening in these pictures? Complete the story by filling in the speech bubbles.

MY COMMITMENT

☐ I will depend on God (not on others) to care for my self-esteem.

☐ I understand that without God I am spiritually lost.

☐ I want God to help me have a humble spirit.

☐ I want God to control my life.

☐ I want God to show me areas of my life where I need to improve.

HAPPINESS IS.....OBEYING GOD

People who get lost in the desert for many days, without food or water, sometimes begin to imagine a beautiful oasis.

A Mirage

1. Did you ever spend a lot of time without food or water? If so, how did you feel? And if not, how do you think you would feel?

2. Did you ever want something so much that you began to imagine or dream that you were already receiving it?

3. Imagine you are in this picture, and you run toward the oasis thinking there is water and food. But you realize that it's just a mirage. How would you feel?

4. Do you think that people seek happiness with the same intensity as someone in the desert who is thirsty seeks water?

WRITE 10!

Write 10 ways that people look for happiness.

Happiness Is...

1.
2.
3.
4.
5.
6.
7.
8.
9.
10.

RIGHTEOUSNESS
What is it?

RIGHTEOUS
Adjective: describes one who does what is right and godly and acts with justice. The righteous person is the one who has a noble character and right and honest conduct. He/she behaves according to the will of God and has a good relationship with him. Sinners who repent and receive justification by faith are made righteous. The grace of God helps you live in righteousness.

RIGHTEOUSNESS
Noun: it is the quality of being good, righteous and fair. The righteousness of God has to do with his redemption.

Write Matthew 5:6 in your own words.

_____ are those who hunger and thirst for _____, for they will be _____.

Blessed are those who hunger and thirst for righteousness, for they will be filled.

(Matthew 5:6)

157

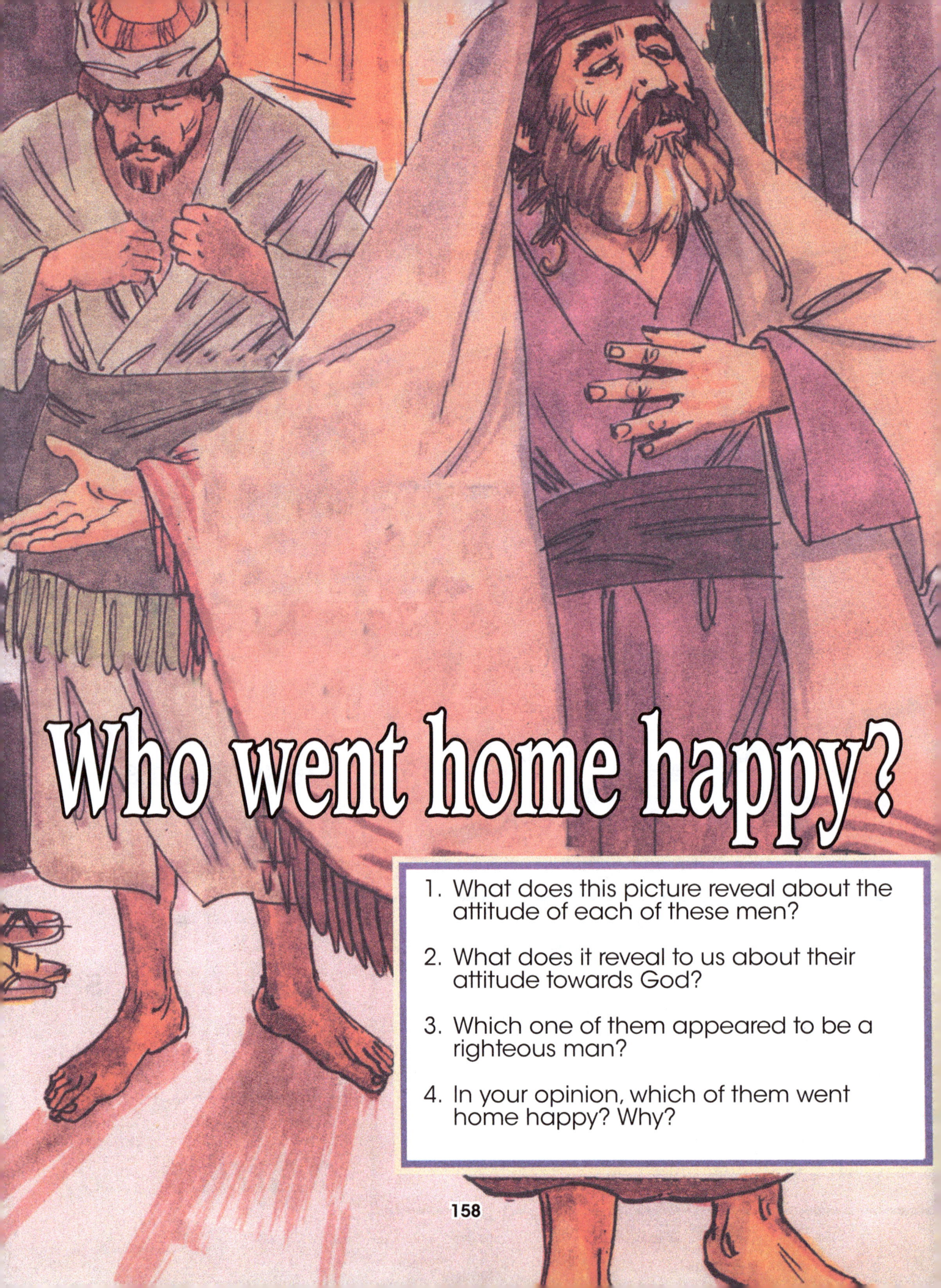

Who went home happy?

1. What does this picture reveal about the attitude of each of these men?

2. What does it reveal to us about their attitude towards God?

3. Which one of them appeared to be a righteous man?

4. In your opinion, which of them went home happy? Why?

SHOULD I FORGIVE?

Forgiveness

WHO NEEDS IT?

?

What is forgiveness?

Who needs to be forgiven?

Why is it hard to forgive others?

What makes you feel better: forgiveness or revenge?

WHAT DOES THE BIBLE SAY ABOUT FORGIVENESS?

Complete the following verses:

"Be_____ and _____ to one another, _____ each other, just as in Christ God _____ you." (Ephesians 4:32)

"And when you stand praying, if you hold anything _____ anyone, _____ them, so that your Father in heaven may _____ you your sins." (Mark 11:25).

"For if you _____ other people when they _____ against you, your _____ Father will also _____ you. But if you do not _____ others their sins, your _____ will not _____ your sins." (Matthew 6:14-15)

"Bear with each other and _____ one another if any of you has a grievance against someone. _____ as the Lord _____ you." (Colossians 3:13).

VICTORIOUS IN CHRIST

HEROES OF JESUS

Describe someone who deserves to be rewarded as a hero for having overcome great difficulties.

TROPHY FOR:

_____

BECAUSE:

_____

_____

_____

_____

WHAT DOES THE BIBLE TELL US?

Cross out the boxes that have a triangle in the corner.

We	cannot	are	not	being	the	first
			last	Christians	people	
a	or	followers	to			persecution
can	facing	friends	good	evil		

(Read Matthew 5:12)

We	all	can	be	feel	at	sad
joy	and	anger	happiness		when	he
we	make	face	always		a	and
thanks		persecution			revelation	

(Read Matthew 5:11-12)

Because	We	are	must	two	pray
and	send	love	hate	all	those
who	try	pray	believe	us	and
i	persecute	cry		us	

(Read Matthew 5:44)

None of these phrases makes sense if we do not compare them with the example of Jesus, who was persecuted and died on the cross.

WHAT WOULD YOU DO IF YOU FACED PERSECUTION?

1.

In your social science class they are talking about heroes. A student says that it is a pity that the heroes die. You comment that Christian heroes continue to live even after death. The teacher looks at you in surprise and asks you, "You don't believe that there is life after death, right?"
What would you do?

2.

A group of students at your school are talking about a classmate that you know is a Christian. They make fun of her because of her beliefs and they want you to join them.
What can you do?

3.

It is 2020 and they are imprisoning Christians for their faith. Suddenly, you learn that some policemen are looking for you.
What would you do?

Design a poster that depicts

Matthew 5:10-12

164

DEFEND YOUR BELIEFS

CHRISTIANS NEVER EVER

[ ]

write an action

UNLESS...

MOST	SOME	NONE	
			Your parents would never find out.
			Your best friends did it and encouraged you to do the same.
			You were offered a lot of money if you did it.
			Everyone would make fun of you if you didn't.
			You had to do it to be part of the group.
			A gang threatened you: "Do it or you will regret it".
			You would lose your life if you didn't.

165

DID Daniel CONFORM?

Read Daniel 1 and answer the following questions

1. What were the responsibilities of the king's officer in training the young Hebrews? (vv 4-5)

2. According to verse 7, what should the young Hebrews be content with?

3. According to verses 5 and 8, what else should they submit to?

4. What test were they given and what were the results? (vv 12-16)

5. How did these young men, who refused to conform, compare to the others? (vv 19-20)

IN WHOM DO YOU TRUST?

WHO DO YOU GO TO WHEN YOU NEED HELP?

When doing homework

_____

When choosing your clothes for a special occasion.

_____

When deciding what to do when someone hurts your feelings.

_____

To learn something you really want to do.

_____

When deciding if an action is Christian or not.

_____

To know what to do if you fail as a Christian.

_____

Did he understand Nebuchadnezzar's vision?

1. Why did the astrologers fail to explain the meaning of Nebuchadnezzar's dream? (Daniel 2: 4-7)

2. What would happen to Daniel if he did not interpret the dream? (vv 12-13)

3. How did Daniel know the meaning of the King's Dream? (vv 17-19)

4. Briefly describe the dream and its meaning (vv.29-45).

5. How did Daniel explain his ability to interpret the dream? (verses 27-28, 45)

6. What did Nebuchadnezzar learn about God?

Rob knows that Eric is behaving badly at home and at school. Last Saturday, he caused a problem at the mall. Rob is trying to decide whether he should continue spending time with Eric.

Can the Bible give Rob any advice?

Use this concordance to find the Bible reference for each verse. Then, look up the verses in your Bible and check to see if they are correct. Make any corrections to any errors you may find.

WISDOM

Gen.	3:6	also desirable for gaining **w**
1 Kgs.	4:29	God gave Solomon **w** and insight
2 Chr.	1:10	Give me **w** and knowledge
Ps.	51:6	you taught me **w**.
	111:10	fear of the Lord is the beginning of **w**
Prv.	2:6	the Lord gives **w**
	3:13	Blessed are those who find **w**
	4:7	beginning of **w** is this
	8:11	for **w** is more precious than rubies
	11:2	with humility comes **w**
	13:10	**w** is found in those who take advice
	23:23	**w**, instruction and insight as well.
	29:3	A man who loves **w** brings joy
	29:15	A rod and a reprimand impart **w**
	31:26	She speaks with **w**
Isa.	11:2	the Spirit of **w** and of understanding
	28:29	whose **w** is magnificent.
Jer.	10:12	he founded the world by his **w**
Mt.	11:19	But **w** is proved right
Lk.	2:52	Jesus grew in **w** and stature
Acts	6:3	known to be full of the Spirit and **w**
Rom.	11:33	Oh, the depth of the riches of the **w**
1 Cor.	1:17	not with **w** and eloquence
	1:30	who has become for us **w**
	12:8	a message of **w w**
Eph.	1:17	may give you the Spirit of **w**
Col.	2:3	are hidden all the treasures of **w**
	2:23	have an appearance of **w**
Jas.	1:5	If any of you lacks **w**, you should ask
Rev.	5:12	to receive power and wealth and **w**

WISE

1 Kgs.	3:12	I will give you a **w** and discerning heart
Job	5:13	He catches the **w** in their craftiness
Ps.	19:7	making **w** the simple
Prv.	3:7	Do not be **w** in your own eyes
	9:8	rebuke the **w** and they will love you
	10:1	A **w** son brings joy to his father
	11:30	the one who is **w** saves lives
	13:1	A **w** son heeds his father's instruction
	13:20	Walk with the **w** and become **w**
	16:23	The hearts of the **w**
	17:28	fools are thought **w** if they keep silent
Ecc.	9:17	The quiet words of the **w**
Jer.	9:23	Let not the **w** boast of their wisdom
Mt.	11:25	hidden these things from the **w**
1 Cor.	1:19	I will destroy the wisdom of the **w**
	1:27	things of the world to shame the **w**
	3:19	He catches the **w**
Eph.	5:15	not as unwise but as **w**
2 Ti.	3:15	which are able to make you **w**
Jam.	3:13	Who is **w** and understanding

Where can you find WISDOM?

Would any of these verses help Rob?

The fear of the Lord is the beginning of wisdom; all who follow his precepts will have a good life.
(   )

I have not stopped giving thanks for you, remembering you in my prayers. I keep asking that the God of our Lord Jesus Christ, the glorious Father, may give you the Spirit of wisdom, so that you may have more knowledge.
(   )

For the Lord gives wisdom; from his mouth come knowledge and understanding.
(   )

If any of you lacks wisdom, you should ask God, who gives generously to all without finding fault, and it will be given to you.
(   )

Walk with the wise and become wise, for a companion of fools gets hurt.
(   )

WHAT KIND OF WISDOM

Does God Give Us?

Read the following list. Cross out what you think God does not promise to give us.

1. A guide to help you decide the right thing.
2. The answers to the exams when you don't study.
3. The ability to know the numbers so that you win the lottery.
4. Guidance so you know when to invite someone to church.
5. Tips on how to get revenge when someone hurts you.
6. Tips on how to forgive someone who's hurt you.

What similarities do you find in the crossed out sentences?

What similarities do you find in the remaining sentences?

Lesson 47

HAVE THE COURAGE TO BE HONEST

I Don't Want to Hear It!

Why don't these preteens want to hear the truth?

Mind your own business!

Leave Me Alone!

It's My Life!

Why don't you look at your own faults?

A Message for Preteens

What warnings and judgments do you think God gives to people today?

In your own words, write on this board some of the messages that God has for preteens today. Use these verses as a reference: Philippians 2:3; Colossians 3:2; Ephesians 6:1-3; Titus 3:1-2; and Deuteronomy 10:12.

The warnings are in the Word of God for all to read, but few heed them.

How can we say
the TRUTH
with love?

Check your attitude

YES	NO	
		Are you talking about the judgment of God (or yours)?
		Do you feel happy when you judge?
		When making a judgment, do you do it with love and to help?
		Can you respond with Christian love even if others do not understand your intentions?

HAVE THE COURAGE TO STAND FIRM

I would do anything for..._____!

PERSECUTION

BEFORE AND NOW

Read Hebrews 11:32-12:3 and answer these questions

1 Who are some of the Old Testament heroes mentioned because of their faith?

2 According to verses 36-38, what types of persecution did they face?

3 In Hebrews 12:1, what does the writer compare to the Christian life?

4 According to Hebrews 12:2, how is Jesus a model for us?

5 In Hebrews 12:3, how does Jesus help those who are facing persecution today?

6 In what ways are Christians persecuted today?

7 How can Christians have the courage to stand firm despite persecution?

"Therefore, since we are surrounded by such a great cloud of witnesses, let us throw off everything that hinders and the sin that so easily entangles. And let us run with perseverance the race marked out for us," *(Hebrews 12:1)*

Lesson 49

GOOD NEWS

GOOD NEWS

"Therefore the Lord himself will give you a sign: The virgin will conceive and give birth to a son, and will call him Immanuel."
(Isaiah 7:14).

Joseph son of David, do not be afraid to take Mary home as your wife, because what is conceived in her is from the Holy Spirit. She will give birth to a son, and you are to give him the name Jesus, because he will save his people from their sins."

All this took place to fulfill what the Lord had said through the prophet: "The virgin will conceive and give birth to a son, and they will call him Immanuel" (which means "God with us").

(Matthew 1:20b-23)

How long did the people wait?

Since the creation of the world, God in his love wanted to have communion with people. When Adam and Eve disobeyed, everything changed. Sin brought as a consequence the need for a Savior. Genesis 3:5 is considered the first prophecy that suggests God's plan to send a special Savior.

Because of the terrible sin of the people, God sent a flood. However, he saved Noah and his family. God spoke with Abraham and promised him that he would bless the whole world through him. Joseph and Mary, Jesus' parents, were descendants of Abraham.

God always cared for his people. He freed them from slavery in Egypt. Then he gave them laws so they would know how they should live. The law showed people their disobedience, and that they could not save themselves.

When the people of God disobeyed, he sent prophets to admonish them. Then, he sent enemy armies to invade them as a way to punish them. Along with the warnings, God made promises of freedom. The prophets told the people that God would send a Messiah or Savior.

After the people of God returned from exile, they spent 400 years without prophets. They only had the promises that God had made years before. Some forgot the promises and stopped trusting in God. However, many continued to wait for the promised Messiah.

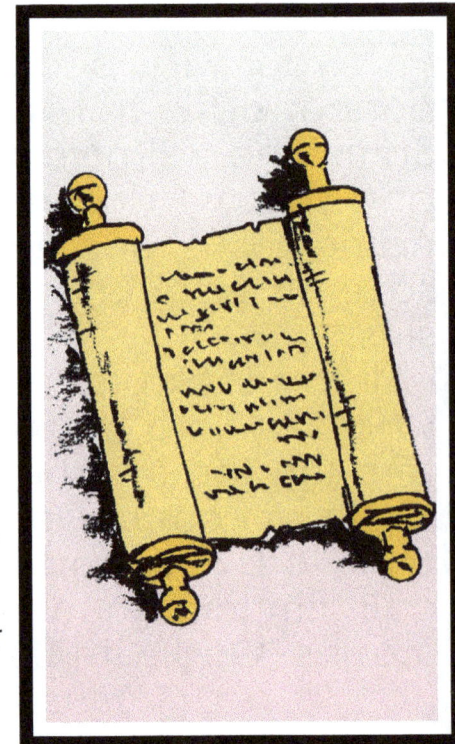

Why did God wait so long?

When Jesus was born, the kingdom of Herod the Great had had peace for a generation. The Jews only took care of their daily responsibilities and their religious rituals.

Taxes were high, but the land was productive. Farmers provided food for large cities; the Sea of Galilee provided a growing fishing industry, and many men worked on Herod's construction projects.

Caesar Augustus brought stability to the Roman Empire. The land and sea routes provided safer travel and communication between the large cities. The emperor supervised, in person, the construction and maintenance of 95,000 kilometers of roads.

Greek was the common language, and the Romans tolerated the practice of different religions. There was a new legal system, and everyone was forced to submit. Officials collected taxes to keep the government functioning.

Nobody knows why God chose that moment to send Jesus. On a human level, it seemed ideal. There was a common language, the routes made it much easier to spread the news quickly. There was an organized form of communication. The government was stable and tolerant of religious ideas. Whatever the reason, God decided it was the right time.

The wait was almost over when...

179

Joseph and Mary were already married.

The angel Gabriel told Mary that she would have a baby.

Gabriel told Mary that the child would be called Joseph.

The power of the Holy Spirit helped Mary become pregnant with Baby Jesus even though she was a virgin.

Joseph was glad when he learned that Mary was pregnant.

Joseph planned to divorce Mary.

An angel told Joseph to take Mary as his wife.

The angel told Joseph that the baby's name would be Jesus.

After this, Joseph and Mary got married.

Read the phrases in the boxes above. Put an X in the boxes that are false and an O in the ones that are true. Reread the incorrect phrases, and change them to be true.

Write a poem

Write a five line poem without rhyme. Follow these instructions:

Line 1: Subject.

Line 2: two adjectives that describe the subject.

Line 3: two verbs or actions about the subject.

Line 4: a six-word comment about the subject.

Line 5: a word that is synonymous with (similar to) the subject.

Isaiah
Faithful,
Trustworthy,
He prayed,
He believed,
He spoke a
message of
hope.
Prophet

Mary

Joseph

Write a poem without rhyme for Mary and one for Joseph.

IT WAS WORTH THE WAIT!

PART OF THE PLAN!

Who Am I? Put my name in the blank.

I had faith and followed God wherever he guided me. I was an ancestor of Jesus.

_____

I was a shepherd and a king. I was an ancestor of Jesus.

_____

An angel told me that I would be the mother of Jesus.

_____

God used the decree that I gave to take a national census. My decree led Joseph and Mary to Bethlehem.

_____

God gave me courage to overcome doubts and cultural traditions. I married a young woman who was pregnant.

_____

THE

THE BETHLEHEM HERALD

Vol. XII

No. 12

THE CENSUS BEGINS

MANGERS FOR SALE

Silas' store has just put his entire inventory of mangers on sale. Many are made with bricks and are very heavy. The weight ensures that they remain in place while the animals eat.

Silas offers the best prices in the area, but does not include home delivery.

Manger's have many different uses. Recently, one was used as a cradle for a baby.

EXPECTED TAX INCREASE

Many citizens were angry about the announcement of the new tax increase. Most of the people we interviewed commented that it will be difficult to meet the basic needs of their family if the government continues to raise taxes. The authorities are faced with a dilemma: request more money for roads and military guard, or listen to the requests of citizens.

The authorities say that someone has to pay for the construction and maintenance of the 95,000 kilometers of roads, and for soldiers who keep the peace and fight crime.

The citizens have no choice. They must pay taxes or they will be arrested.

NO VACANCIES

The roads are full of thousands of travelers who are returning to their places of birth for the census. The figures indicate that a large part of the population is obeying the decree of Caesar Augustus to participate in the census.

There are large crowds on all of the roads in the country. Many have traveled for days. Some show signs of fatigue. Those who have friends or family in Bethlehem are the ones who are most excited about the trip.

The Chamber of Commerce reports that visitors have flooded the city. All the hotels are full. Owners of private houses that have agreed to accommodate some visitors say that they no longer have space for anyone else. Some people find themselves sleeping in stables, caves or on the street. The Chamber of Commerce will meet in two weeks to decide if it is necessary to build more shelters.

It is reported that a family visiting for the census had their first baby. They named him Jesus.

Because of the housing problem, the baby's parents sought refuge in a stable and the baby was born there. They are using a manger as a bed. The mother and the baby are in good health.

PATIENCE, PLEASE!

Read each letter and write an answer, encouraging preteens to patiently wait for God's work in their lives.

Dear Patience:

I'm in sixth grade and I'm tired of school. And I still have many years of study! I do not think I can take it anymore. I'm sure I will not go to college. I would like to be old enough to work and earn my own money. Would God like me to leave school and start working?
Sincerely,
Bored

Dear Bored:

Sincerely,
Patience

Dear Patience:

I am a new Christian and I am excited to learn about God. I would like all my friends to decide to follow Jesus too, but they aren't interested. I can't lead anyone to Christ. I don't believe that I'm a good witness for Christ.
Sincerely,
Failed

Dear Failed:

Sincerely,
Patience

Dear Patience:

I always hear that God has plans for everyone's life, but maybe he has forgotten mine. Nothing exciting happens to me. I pray every day, but nothing special happens in my life.
Sincerely,
Always the same

Dear Always the same:

Sincerely,
Patience

HOW THE GOOD NEWS IS DELIVERED

GUESS WHAT HAPPENED!

Complete the phrases:

The happiest day of my life was when...

I want to tell my best friend...

My parents never saw me as excited as when...

185

PROCLAIM
The Good News

Read Luke 2: 16-18, 20. Write in your own words what you think the shepherds told people about the baby Jesus and the message the angels gave them.

Many people today seem to always be in a hurry, so if you want to leave a message you must be brief.

Can you think of a way to tell the good news about Jesus to people who are in a hurry?

Try to write a message with just a few words. Write two-line phrases that express the truth about Jesus and the joy of knowing him. Here are some examples.

Jesus is the only Son of God. Living for him makes my heart beat faster.

God sent Jesus to earth to give us love and eternal life.

GOOD NEWS FOR Today's BUSY PEOPLE

How will I tell others?

A LONG TRIP TO SEE A KING

What is Myrrh?

Myrrh: an expensive and aromatic plant. It was used to prepare perfume, incense, and to embalm the bodies of the deceased before their funeral. Myrrh was imported from Arabia and India. Since it was a luxury product, it was an appropriate gift for a king, as were the gold and incense that the wise men from the east brought to the baby Jesus.

MYRRH

Psalm 45: 8	robes are fragrant with **m** and aloes and cassia…
Matthew 2:11	presented him with gifts of gold, frankincense and **m**
Mark 15:23	Then they offered him wine mixed with **m**
John 19: 39-40	Nicodemus brought a mixture of **m** and aloes
Rev. 18:13	cargoes of cinnamon and spice, of incense, **m** and frankincense

Use this concordance to answer the following questions:

1. Who brought myrrh to the baby Jesus?

2. How was myrrh offered to Jesus on the cross?

3. For what did Nicodemus use myrrh after Jesus died?

MORE THAN A NAME

Use the letters of Jesus' name to make an acrostic about what you know about the Son of God.

J

E

S

U

S

Now, with the letters of your name, make an acrostic that indicates ways you can learn more about Jesus.

How can a preteen receive Jesus as his or her personal savior?

REVIEW OF UNIT XI

1. Admit you have sinned

2. Repent of your sins (say you're sorry)

3. Decide that you will stop sinning.

4. Ask God to forgive you for your sins.

Build your relationship with God through prayer, reading the Bible and attending church.

The more time you spend with Jesus, the better your relationship with him will be.

Review of Unit XI

Who were the Old Testament prophets who announced the birth of Jesus?

Who will you tell the Good News about Jesus to?

Tell about some of the time of Jesus' birth, that made the ideal.

How does this phrase apply to the lessons of the unit: "It Was Worth the Wait"?

Tell about some of the reactions people had when they met Jesus.

What did these lessons teach you about trust in God?

Insert the tip of a pencil through a paper clip and place it in the middle of the circle. Spin the paper clip, and answer the question that the clip stops on. Continue until you have answered all the questions.